MORNING CANDLE

The Mind Matters Collection

Tabi Upton

ISBN: 1517498767
ISBN 13: 9781517498764

For Mammoo and Daddoo,
who waited for this collection with great excitement and joy

It was great meeting
you in Kauai!

11/2016

CONTENTS

FOREWORD

The life of the mind involves human experiences amplified by reason. For more than a decade, columnist Tabi Upton used a therapist's ear and a journalist's pen to craft opinion columns published in the Life section of the Chattanooga Times Free Press. Sometimes her pieces were deeply personal, other times they were shared anecdotes about the people she met in the formative years of the 21st century.

Her topics ranged from the single life, to the nature of friendship, to understanding family dynamics. Her writer's voice is that of a caring friend, and newspaper readers responded enthusiastically to her real-life stories and gentle encouragement.

Not only can Upton make words line up and march, but she also practices the first rule of good writing: show, don't tell. Rather and pontificate on topics of the heart, she uses simple words and everyday situations to share parables about better living.

The results were columns that her editors considered gifts to readers. Please share in those gifts in the pages that follow, and remember that, in all we do, our minds matter.

-- Mark Kennedy, The Chattanooga Times Free Press Newspaper

INTRODUCTION

There is a lovely couple that I've known most of my life. The Sutherlands live in a beautiful and simple log house on the side of Lookout Mountain, a woodsy foothill that sits between Tennessee and Georgia. The green and imposing forest surrounding their home hides a bubbling creek nearby, but the sound of its fresh water is often just noticeable on the wind. There are large rocks, flowers, and fruit trees scattered about. And of course, a dog or two always barks a welcome or a warning to them of visitors. The wife, gifted in hospitality, loves to have people come for breakfast, lunch or dinner. She then treats them like royalty.

There will be a table laden with jams and homemade bread, soups, hot teas, fresh flowers, and *always* peaceful lighting. Once, at a beautiful breakfast at her house, her morning candles startled me. I had always associated candles with the closing of the day, never with the beginning. I remember commenting to her about those sweet morning candles, which seemed completely normal from her point of view, but were extravagant from mine.

The vision of that surprising and tentative light in the early morning has stuck with me for years. To me it symbolizes hope for the possibilities ahead and an expression of beauty and heartfelt indulgence in the now, regardless of whatever else the day brings. I want my writing to offer that kind of hope. I want it to be a small beginning of things yet unseen, a positive outlook for what could happen later on this day, this week, or this year.

My column, *Mind Matters*, ran in the Chattanooga Times Free Press in Chattanooga, Tennessee from 2001 to 2013. I have gathered my favorite ones through the years into one place, a place to quiet our hearts, laugh, reflect, and become better people, friends, and family. I hope you will find encouragement, motivation, insight, raw honesty, and joy in these little candles.

PART I
MORNING CANDLE

"We can easily forgive a child who is afraid of the dark; the real tragedy of life is when men are afraid of the light."
— Plato

1

GIVING GRACE

The other day I was admiring a shirt a young friend was wearing.

"I know who that shirt would look really good on," I remarked, then with a chuckle added, "I could buy it for him, but he doesn't deserve it."

My young friend paused and then said, "Buy it for him anyway. Give him grace." I was stunned. Give grace? When it's left to us, most of us aren't naturally graceful. We tend to give based on what we think other people have given to us. We withhold when we feel they have hurt us, taken from us or simply not given much to fill our own love tanks. I've been thinking about the mysterious gift of grace lately — not just toward strangers in need but also to those we know pretty well and feel don't deserve it.

It seems in order to do this well we must recognize and reflect on the grace we have received. I've told the story before of the day my love of chocolate got the best of me. I was in first grade and selling candy bars for a school fundraiser. I ate half of one without paying for it and then hid it behind the trash can. My father found it, and asked simply, "Why didn't you just eat it all?"

I think he recognized that guilt had overcome my passion for chocolate; and in my childish manner, I had repented by leaving it where someone could find it. I received no extra punishment for my crime. He gave me grace.

A vocal, yet responsible teen, I remember not going to class one day to prepare for a sanctioned school activity. One teacher didn't know the details and had gone looking for me. When I dropped by my class briefly again, my classmates warned me that I was probably in trouble. I replied with a torrent of attitude.

"I already have permission to go and he can't stop me 'cause the principal already said it was fine and I don't care what he says..." Suddenly, my classmates simultaneously suffered a coughing attack. I turned to see my teacher standing behind me, listening quietly. He steadily dismissed me to my activity. When I returned with slightly more humility, he said nothing about my disrespect. He gave me grace.

Aaahh, grace! I could go on. I've been given grace in friendship, in love, in family matters, in work settings, by complete strangers, with children, and by God. I have experienced many situations when things could have gone really wrong but strangely did not. Grace appears to cover the awkward and ungraceful, humbling and disgraceful moments of our lives, whispering that even though we didn't deserve that good thing, we got it anyway. And though we really deserved this bad thing, we won't receive it this time. If we listen closely, we hear it urging us to pass that same experience along to others.

There are moments when justice must be served. There are many times when we really ought to pay our own consequences, learning and growing from the stinging rebuke. Sometimes, though, it's wonderful to receive and to offer a little gift of grace.

So yes, I bought the shirt.

2

A WARM BLANKET

Zella Dixon didn't want to write a book. She fought the soft voice that spoke to her one morning during her prayer and meditation time that said, "I want you to write." Like Moses, she questioned the call.

"Me, write, Lord? I can't even speak well," she thought.

Hard of hearing and dyslexic, Dixon was an unlikely writer. She thought her brother, musical and intellectually gifted and good with words, would have made a better candidate. Stranger still, after her first humble attempt, her book manuscript was lost twice. Each time she'd breathed a sigh of relief, and each time it was miraculously found and returned to her.

Dixon could not refuse her destiny. So now, at age 78, her book, "A Warm Blanket for Rainy Days," written with local author Dean Arnold, tells the story of her life of many joys and sorrows, some incredibly difficult losses, some intense storms. Each time she lost a beloved person, she seemed to receive from God a supernatural comfort that lay like a warm blanket upon her. Her message of love and hope is that our loved ones are never truly gone from us.

Her young life had not seen much trouble. Reared in Johnson City, Tenn., in a home with love, traditional values and deep family connections, she shared a room with her grandmother until her marriage at age 18. She fell head-over-heels for her husband, Sherwin, a handsome professional baseball player with a kind heart who drew children to him like the Pied Piper. They settled into a wonderful life in Miami and had three children, two boys and a girl. The revolution of the 1960s took its toll on one of her boys, who struggled with substance abuse and alcoholism. The other made money easily and became successful in jewelry making.

Her daughter gave the perfect balance to the trio. One night, Dixon's mother was up late, unable to sleep, when she saw her daughter-in-law on the stairs, surrounded by an oval light. She told Dixon's mom, "I've just come to tell you that everything will be all right."

The daughter-in-law had died two years earlier. It was after this vision that the losses began. Several family members died over the course of a few months, and there were more as the years passed. Each one tugged at a different part of the heart, forcing those left behind to come to grips with their helplessness and humanity.

Dixon remembered those words and learned that God had already sent His comfort in the most trying of times. A deeply spiritual woman, she has read a devotional every morning for the past 50 years, and so it was only fitting that her story be told in this form. There are meditations that will strike deeply, like the very first one, titled, "You Get Stronger When You Know You Can Handle Whatever Life Has To Bring." Or No. 35, "Self-Knowledge Is Very Painful, Most of Us Prefer the Illusion." In No. 38, she writes, "Through my inner journey … I've learned that I do have a voice. I can speak."

No. 43, about former local news anchorwoman MaryEllen Locher who succumbed to cancer a few years ago, stunned me and brought tears to my eyes. Dixon has given facials to clients at a local salon for many years. She can tell a lot about what's going on in a person by analyzing their facial skin.

The treatment she gave Locher went beyond a beauty ritual. Locher wrote her a note praising her ability to turn a facial into a deep spiritual experience. This devotional begins in light and ends in light, reminding us that in the midst of our darkest times, there is still a refuge to cling to.

3

ACCIDENTAL GARDEN YIELDS SURPRISES

Life is full of surprises. One of my greatest surprises one year was my beautiful, wild, verdant and accidental garden. It was built as a comfort gift from my father during my recovery from foot surgery. He brought in railroad ties and positioned them along one side of my garage. Then he filled the area with dirt and manure. Family, friends, helpful guests and I all randomly tossed in vegetable refuse. I added leftover fibers from my juice machine. There were banana peels, apple skins, lettuce, greens, melon rinds, potato skins, beans and onions involved in the process. I might have put whole but rotting veggies in also, complete with seeds.

I lamented that I was late in planting it. I bought a few seeds from the store, took a few from my parents' stash and tried to plan a date to begin. I kept checking to see if it wasn't already too late to plant. I didn't want to waste time planting if the summer sun was going to kill the emerging growth anyway. I wondered if I shouldn't just wait till the next year. Then one day, a couple of neighbors walked by and asked me what was growing in my garden.

"Weeds," I responded matter-of-factly. I shook my head sadly. My garden stood lonely and neglected. I should tend it soon, I thought, before it begins to look just like my lawn, a carpet of grass. I finally determined to get my hands dirty. As I bent to pull out the green invaders, I noticed what did look like small seedlings growing up amid the grass stalks. I left them alone, but I still didn't return to plant. A week later, there were more seedlings growing. I wondered if someone had planted in my honor, but the random scattering did not appear to have been deliberate.

As the weeks flew by, the plants grew up so thick you could not see the dirt between them, and they vined and snaked wildly, spilling out over the railroad ties. Bright yellow flowers appeared on some of them, and then finally, triumphantly, the fruit of nature's labor.

I identified three types of tomatoes: Roma, Big Boy and grape. I discovered that tomatoes grow just fine trailing along the earth. I saw a small cantaloupe appear, then a striped melon. I was ecstatic. I made a tomato salad, filling it in with fresh oregano leaves, olives and carrots. I topped it off with vinaigrette and delighted in the produce.

I picked another bowl full of tomatoes, then fried a crisp green one that tasted fresh and perfect. I lifted up leaves to search for more surprises under the greenery. I took pictures of it to send to friends around the country. "You won't believe it, but I didn't officially plant any of this," I'd text. Everyone oohed and ahhed.

My parents came to gaze on this accidental gain. Avid gardeners themselves, they told me I had four cantaloupes, a small watermelon and lots and lots of tomatoes. My mother laughed and said, "Your daddy's jealous! He's not going to bother planting anymore. He'll just throw old veggies out like you did."

The truth was that everyone just loved the surprise.

4

SPIRITUALITY OF DANCE
LIFTS PEOPLE

I like to dance. My favorite place for rhythmic expression is my dining-room floor. I like to shimmy to Latin rhythms while doing housework. I sometimes exercise with my "Dancing with the Stars" DVD, or I'll slide through the kitchen for a playful uplift.

The use of dance has recently soared in the fitness world, and the health benefits are many. Physically, dancing can tighten one's abs, burn flab, and create dramatic, muscular physiques. As a creative expression, it can be used to entertain and expand one's awareness of beauty and art. Dance can also empower one's inner self. Dancing can have a profound effect on emotions, can be used as a form of worship, and can be a powerful healing activity.

In Eastern cultures, dance is used to impart blessing, overcome emotional problems, even to meditate. One of the most fascinating of these dances is called the *guedra*, which originated with the Blue People of the Tuareg Berber, a nomadic group in North Africa. Living in the southwestern deserts of Morocco, they are called the blue people because they dye their clothes with a deep blue color that rubs off and sinks into their skin. The dance begins with the simple rhythmic beating of a drum and progresses from hand movements to upper body motion and undulation. It is considered a joyful and often hypnotic dance.

Belly dance, often misinterpreted today as a seductive type of dance, has Middle Eastern roots. Originally designed as a celebration of woman's life-giving abilities, it was taught to women before giving birth to reduce pain and ease the entire experience. A woman's friends and family danced around her to encourage her to do the moves during labor. Cathy Moore, a midwife who also became a belly dancer before understanding the connection, read that many of the moves in Lamaze were identical to those taught in belly dance. When she observed what women naturally did to facilitate the birthing process, she realized that these moves were also part of belly dance.

"Because, at its ancient roots, belly dance tells the story of woman's life-giving power, it is a natural for pregnant women who are at the peak of their creative power," she said. "Through belly dance, a woman celebrates her fertility, sensuality, and abundance and affirms the fullness of her being." These amazing roots eventually gave way to the performance dance we are familiar with today.

In Western church history, the Shakers, an offshoot of the Quakers, were given to morality and worship, which they did so fervently that their bodies shook rhythmically. Today, many churches incorporate liturgical or praise dancing into their services as a useful spiritual outlet.

More recently, dance therapy is used in the healing arts to improve self-awareness and interpersonal interaction, providing an outlet for individuals to communicate feelings. It also can reduce stress and muscle tension.

Dance is powerful and can incorporate all aspects of an individual. Whether used for a workout, prayer, celebration or healing agent, dance can be a useful part of living a joyful and vibrant life.

5

A TRIP TO GRANDMA AND GRANDPA'S

A few years ago, I volunteered to transport two of my nephews, Marvin Jr. and Tristian, to my parents' home in Spring City, Tenn., for a weekend visit. Tristian, four at the time, was tall, with hair that sat like golden scribbles atop his head. Marvin, five then, was more compact, with eyes that carried so much emotion they could make a grown man cry. The two bickered like a married couple but loved each other deeply.

I must confess something. I don't usually listen closely to young children's conversations. But the conversations they had that weekend were different. There were particular sound bites that caught my attention. Later, as I reflected, I realized that I could take at least five lessons from what these two children had to say.

> At first the constant screaming was enough to make me pull over to the side of the road and announce firmly, "We'll drive again when it's quiet." Tristian, who is highly verbal, bold and perpetually happy, laughed at me.
>
> "Can you two be quiet!?" I demanded. Marvin, quieter in nature, responsive, and sensitive, broke in with "Yes." Tristian agreed. I drove on.

While playing with miniature men and floppy animal toys in the back seat, they discussed the fact that one day they would grow up to be fathers. "We're getting stronger every year," Tristian informed Marvin. "Yep." Marvin replied. Later, they measured each other to see how close they were to their goals.

Lesson 1: *Look forward to the next phases of life.*
Upon arrival at the house, we gathered our stuff and prepared to go inside. Suddenly, Marvin, Jr. announced, "Your car smells good. It smells like...dried seaweed." He was serious. My sister has exposed him and his sisters to almost every food known to mankind, and it shows. "Whatever, Man," I thought.

Lesson 2: *Receive all compliments gracefully, even the unusual ones.*
As I was washing my car the next morning, I asked if Tristian and Marvin wanted to "help" me. Marvin decided to sleep in, but Tristian joined me. Rather than rinse my car, however, he dragged a large toy car over and began to spray it down alongside mine. Then he began to question me.

"Hey, why are you always at my grandma and grandpa's house and around my cousins?" I looked at him strangely. "Because grandma and grandpa are my mommy and daddy." The connection finally clicked. "Oh." He went on to tell me his parents' names.

"Yes, your daddy is my brother, and grandma and grandpa are his parents too," I explained. He got it. The mystery of why I was always showing up at family gatherings was finally solved, and perhaps he even understood the word "aunt" now. This from a child who already comprehends the concept of a joke and has several memorized.

Lesson 3: *Know your family members.*
The ground was slick and muddy under the carport, and Tristian fell hard while transporting a mop to some random place out front.

"Are you OK?" I wondered out loud. He didn't answer.

Rather than lean on me, he asked, "Where's grandma? " And went looking for her in the front yard by the lake. After all, he needed professional comfort, which was more than I could provide. He recognized I was an amateur.

Lesson 4: *Everybody needs a haven, a place of hugs.*
Later, I brought back a pumpkin from my jungle-like garden. Tristian and Marvin had just returned from feeding grass to maggots under my father's turkey cages. I told Tristian I would give him a pumpkin, also. "Tristian loves pumpkins," I explained to Mom. Tristian chimed in, "I don't just love pumpkins. I love pumpkin pie, pumpkin cake, pumpkin seeds — not just the pumpkin!" OK. But that brings me to my fifth and final lesson.

5. *Find pleasure in the simple things of life.* That weekend, I sure did.

6

KEEP YOUR SENSE OF WONDER

Sometimes things get old. I mean they get boring, predictable, mundane. The piece of art you were wild about when you bought it from the gallery no longer brings pleasure. The spouse you were so in love with on your wedding day no longer causes the heart to beat wildly. Things settle down. And when they do, we lose touch with that passionate part of us that wants to see things with the freshness of childhood.

When I was a teenager, I wrote a poem about wanting to see ordinary things like green grass and blue sky with a sense of wonder. I like the thrill of finding beauty in unexpected places. In Africa, where the Arab influence showed itself in the ritual of afternoon tea, I once gasped at the startling beauty of a cup of sparkling white sugar and a pile of deeply green, fresh mint leaves, hugging up to the steaming pot of caramel-colored tea.

In college, I can remember being moved to tears by words, art and current events. And then, practicality moved in. Things got old, regular, ordinary. Most of us have heard the popular song with this famous line, " ... I hope you never lose your sense of wonder ..." We long to keep it. But we seldom can. One reason is that most of us are so caught up in doing that we fail to simply be.

To enjoy the beauty of the ordinary things, one must be fully present in the moment. I tend to pack my schedule so that I am engaged in something during most of my waking moments. At first I am buoyed by the sense of urgency, of movement, of meaning. Then I begin to go to sleep thinking of what I need to do the next day. Within a matter of weeks, I can predict where I'll be mentally. Life will have dulled out to a meaningless rush from one event to the next.

I will feel like I'm on a roller coaster that has lost its screaming power. And I will miss simple pleasures. When I finally get a day to myself, I'll spend it in quietness — walking outside, picking wildflowers and pretty weeds, smelling honeysuckle, reading magazines and reflecting. I'll start planning more time to simply be, and then life rises up in full color again.

We sometimes miss wonder when we uncover mystery too soon. I was reminded of this when a young friend of mine told me about his first kiss. He was 16, which is late by today's standards. He wrote a poem about it: "My heart is now worth giving/My sun is worth shining/My wings are worth flying/My wounds are now healing/I know this because I have kissed beauty."

Many of his peers have had several intimate partners, and they no longer consider a kiss anything special. The slang teenagers are using to describe the incredibly tender and intimate act of passionate love gives evidence to the lost sense of wonder and incredulity that ought to be there. Things that are kept mysterious until that sacred union of "the right place and the right time" keep their sense of wonder. Passion stored is like dynamite.

We keep awe in our lives when we expect to be taken aback from time to time. Life is full of surprises, of interesting twists and turns. A girl who is hardly ever asked out on a date suddenly meets the man of her dreams and marries. The job that felt like backbreaking drudgery gets jumpstarted again when someone is genuinely helped by the service provided. If we allow ourselves to be swept up in the drama around us, if we see life that way, we won't miss those moments of wonder. We will continue to be amazed.

7

POOR IS THE NEW RICH

W e're terrified of the word. Many of us grew up this way and have spent our entire adult lives beating it from our doorways. We remember the fear, the helplessness and the frustration-- of being *poor*. As the economic crisis falls like a wet blanket on our souls, the issues of loss and struggle have risen anew. As a nation, we've enjoyed the wealth and ease that has set us apart from most of the world. We love to shop and couldn't care less if we need the items we buy. We give away what some would dream to have. We eat and eat, while others go hungry.

Even our poverty looks different from that in other parts of the world. In this city, you can be without a house and a job and still eat semi-regularly, get some level of medical attention and have a change of clothes. The food may be old and cold, the medical attention may not be cutting edge, the clothes most likely will be worn, but they are thankfully within reach.

A friend of mine once remarked jovially, "We were poor growing up, but we didn't know it." Well, Buddy, I knew I was poor. When you can see the road from the hole in the bottom of your family's car, you're not deluded. When you watch your daddy painfully count out the change for your lunch money, adding whatever pennies he can find, you become aware. When you can't wait for your sister to take her outfit off so you can wear it to school the next day, something tells you that you may not have as much as others.

Though my poorness was difficult at times, it still was not awful. I attended private school for part of my childhood, traveled and enjoyed many educational enrichments. I ate every day. I lived in a house. My father finally got rid of the Flintstone car and got one with an intact floor. Now we can laugh about those memories.

My father said we were a poor family with middle-class values. He taught his children not to be ashamed of not having and to never let the lack of money stop us from doing whatever we wanted, because desire and effort can make a way. He taught us about other kinds of wealth.

I know a woman who has not worked in several years because of cancer and a brain tumor. She is the thriftiest person I know. When she needs clothes, she sends out e-mails to her friends and lets them know she is looking for any items they no longer want. They leave them in bags on her front door. An anonymous person pays her rent. Her family brings her food. She attended a private college. She went to school a semester, then worked a semester. She graduated with little to no debt. She rarely complains, and she makes her life work. She is tough as nails, and I admire her greatly.

What will our newfound poverty teach us? We can learn to lean a little harder on each other and ask for help. We can reach out to those who have less, like those in biblical times who deliberately left grain in their fields for the poor to pick up and eat. We have been independent, and we have grown fat. The lean years have come. We can grow rich in new ways: in friendship, interdependence, sharing life, laughter, spirituality, hope and faith. Let's indulge.

8

GOING GREEN GRADUALLY

Going green doesn't happen overnight. My quest for cleaner water, food, and ultimately a cleaner planet, has been a gradual shift. I remember drinking tap water like it was going out of style. Once, while overseas and far from civilization, I am ashamed to say that I drank water from an unfamiliar river. And I'd heard of recycling, of course, but in the frenzy of work, social engagements and other obligations, who had time?

Through the years, however, the facts have begun to add up. We now have evidence that plain tap water sometimes contains unwanted elements such as traces of prescription drugs and unwanted chemicals. The situation is similar for the food we eat. Someone challenged me years ago to read the labels of everything I buy. I was mainly searching for excessive amounts of carbohydrates and fats, but I soon discovered that most processed food is made with lots of artificial ingredients. It means that we are ingesting things that our Maker never intended for us to eat, and our bodies cannot digest them properly.

Once, while shopping for pre-packaged oatmeal, I became frustrated that it took me a fairly long time to find a brand that read "all natural." I don't eat organic food all the time, but I do currently look for all-natural and sometimes organic basics like meats, milk, eggs and sometimes apples and carrots. Fortunately many grocery stores are making these options available. I am trying to cook more whole foods rather than the quicker, less satisfying alternatives.

I now filter my water. I still love my snacks, but ironically, have found that some potato and corn chips and sweets aren't made with preservatives of any kind and are more nutritionally dense than certain brands of cereal. Though recycling has been pushed for decades, I did not actively engage in it until recently. It began with my newspapers, and then I decided to try plastics. I work to make it easy. I put a paper bag on my back porch and when I consume juices, I toss the plastic bottles in the bag. I put the newspapers in another bag.

When they're full, I dump them into a container in my garage. When that spills over onto the floor, I take it to the recycling center. Again, it is imperfect, and sometimes I throw away items I could recycle, but the point is that now I am consciously trying to recycle when possible.

I've also noticed that I own quite a collection of colorful and sturdy cloth bags that I have gathered from conferences and special mail offers. I remembered seeing people shop with these types of bags at health-food stores. I decided to try. I'll have to admit, it was a little embarrassing to hand my bags to the Wal-Mart cashier to fill up. She simply smiled and obliged me graciously.

Again, this is hit or miss. When I remember to use my cloth bags, especially for quick, small purchases, I feel a sense of accomplishment. When I forget, I don't worry about it. And that's what I've learned. We must toss out the all-or-nothing thinking. If we can just do better than we did a year ago, that is wonderful progress. Caring for our bodies and our planet starts with the gradual raising of our awareness and taking baby steps toward changing old habits. As always, it is about love: loving this green, beautiful planet, loving health and wellbeing, and loving to do our part to make the world a little better for all of us.

9

SINGING YOURSELF HAPPY

Who hasn't noticed the look of rapture, passion and sheer peace in the faces of the famous children who sing at Public School 22 in New York City? (Google them now if you've never seen them.) You're not just drawn to their amazing voices; you're drawn to their irresistible energy. We've heard about the benefits of music, but did you know that the benefits of singing are also striking? Singing benefits humans emotionally, physiologically, socially and mentally.

You might remember this scenario from childhood: You want to ask your mother something important. You're waiting for just the right moment, knowing if she's cranky or in a hurry the answer will be an automatic "no." You hear her softly singing to herself, and immediately take your opportunity. The sound of someone singing signals the listener that all is well with that person. They are happy and at ease and open for approach.

Singing can cure the blues faster than a pill. You can literally sing your worries out loud, which is done through blues and traditional country-western musical genres. But simply singing to lift anxiety and sadness is often enough to distract yourself from pain and stress. Beth Lawrence, CEO of Viva La Voice! insists that singing promotes deep breathing and oxygenates the blood. There's even evidence that it stimulates brain activity and releases the "feel good" hormones while promoting creativity and improving one's memory.

As a child, I sang with my siblings and neighbors to pass the time when we were bored. We made up songs or learned new ones together, often performing them for our parents and later for others. I still remember phrases of songs I learned in elementary school, and some were in different languages. We all know that if we create a tune for something we want to memorize, it makes it easier. Singing also improves your speaking voice, poise, and posture, giving you confidence to stand before crowds with more ease.

You might believe that singing is best reserved for those with a talent for it. John Lennon, professor emeritus of vocal performance at Emporia State University in Kansas, thinks everyone can and should sing.

"... Human sound is the mind resonating through the instrument of the body," he said. "I contend that singing is an inborn response in those moments of absolute emotional tranquility. Babies sing to themselves.

"The fact that we recognize no identifiable melodic sequence does not mean that it is not singing. Such spontaneous oral response has sustained emission, rhythm, pitch variation and emotional expression. Like the infant, we sing because we feel good and singing makes us feel even better.

"When we sing to ourselves we are, in effect, communicating with the inner self ... It may well be counter-productive to one's well-being not to sing." Singing boosts one's immunity and prolongs life. Seniors who sing show decreased signs of depression and used less medication in one study. It even improves us socially. Remember the spontaneous explosions of singing in malls around the country during the holidays?

These were thrilling to watch and a joy to experience. Singing connects us to others in a way that is unique, warm, and easily received.

10

HIKING

If life is a journey, it is often a hike. A set of unlikely, brief hikes that are strangely connected — like the hikes I've taken recently. The first was with my trusty friend and co-worker who is always game for something new. The day began with a promising coolness. We hiked a trail looking for a waterfall, and then split up to find it or a secondary way out. I walked straight up a hill trying to break free of the trail and find a quicker escape route. She walked on, hoping to come to the end of the trail that way. Instead, we both reappeared huffing and puffing with no choice but to turn back. And then I noticed the clouds — dark, hovering, and looking like they meant business.

With just 15 minutes remaining in our walk, the rain began to pour down, drenching us to the skin. Lightening flashed around us in threatening sparks, vision blurred, the sky was dark. It could have made us miserable. Instead, we decided it was a true adventure. When we completed the hike and arrived back at the car, we soon forgot our brush with danger and went to look at nice houses in quaint neighborhoods. Perhaps it was denial of what we'd been through. Perhaps we simply realized that life goes on.

The next time we took a group of girls hiking with us. They were urban-dwellers — most had never been on a hike; one swore we were killing her. We started at the same point, but didn't take them quite as far. After all, they weren't quite ready. Several carried bags of chips with them, which they munched absentmindedly as they walked along. The others discussed boyfriend issues, some laughed unsupportively at the one straggler. We stopped at the overlook and discussed what hiking could teach us, but no one commented much. They stared out blankly, probably thinking of other things, ready for a snack. It was a very different hike, yet, we all made it out.

Then I hiked again with the child of one of my best friends. The day was unusually warm, and just as pretty. Rachael was small, wiry, and motivated. She hiked behind me and then led me back. She outpaced the other adults on the trail, and encouraged me with, "We can't give up!" I was proud of her. It was like passing the baton to someone more able to take this hike, someone who did it with such energy and freshness I was amazed all over again at the beauty of spirit, of passion, of life.

You just never know what to expect on any given hike. I remember hiking at summer camp with my cabin mates, feeling mischievous and carefree. In college, I hiked a mountain just as the sun was going down. I was terrified the night would find me still walking in the woods, where wild pigs roamed. I was once accosted by a crazy man while hiking overseas. He stood in my path and would not let me by. He growled at me and reached toward me. I lunged away, screaming. Others came to rescue me. But still I hike.

You cannot predict how the hike will go, just like life. We learn along the way, we take the good with the bad, we enjoy the view. We take in the beauty around us, push through the storm, and avoid the dangerous people if we can. We suck in our breath when we are afraid and we speed up across menacing places.

We enjoy hiking with others. And somehow, at some point, we all make it out.

PART II
INTERESTING PEOPLE, FARAWAY PLACES, & CRAZY ANIMALS

"The earth laughs in flowers."
— Ralph Waldo Emerson

11

HORSE STORY

A few years ago I took a personal retreat for the weekend to rest and write. I spent it in a cabin near a lake where horses were grazing. I sat on the porch one afternoon to sing. I got carried away and closed my eyes for a while. When I opened them, several horses were gathered in a semicircle around me in rapt attention. I was completely caught off guard. I felt we'd somehow traversed an unspoken animal-human barrier and that, if they had begun asking me intelligible questions at that moment, it would not have been as shocking then as it may have been in a different setting.

Feeling strangely self-conscious, I thanked them for coming and politely excused myself, shuffling back inside the cabin. From a window I watched as the horses slowly returned to grazing as if nothing had happened. The magic faded. Linda Kohanov, an equine trainer, rider, lecturer and writer, believes that horses have complex abilities to sense and mirror emotion and help assist humans in better understanding their own. For example, trainers like her and Ariana Strozzi both write amazing stories of situations where horses who have worked with individuals with multiple personality disorder quickly shifted their behavior as each persona in a woman manifested.

In another leadership session using horses, one woman had trouble taking control of her life because she believed all leaders were angry and abusive. When she began working with horses, she herself became angry and mean, revealing the same tendency within herself she had fought hard to sublimate. Recently, I joined a group of local therapists at Rock Bluff Stables atop Lookout Mountain to participate in an equine therapy session. Led by Georgianna Pollock and Erin Rayburn, this form of equine therapy is used all over the world for emotional growth and learning. Both these women are passionate about horses and have worked with them since childhood. They believe horses are amazing creatures.

"They are incredibly intuitive and aware of their surroundings," Rayburn states. "Often they mirror the dynamic of a group of humans or an individual. You can't lie to a horse. They meet you exactly where you are in that moment." According to Rayburn, equine therapy "is an experiential process ... participants learn about themselves and others by participating in activities with horses. [Afterward] they discuss their thoughts, beliefs, behaviors, and patterns. It's effective because of the dynamic interplay between horses and humans that requires developing life skills such as nonverbal communication, assertiveness, creative thinking, problem-solving, leadership, responsibility, teamwork and attitude. This often then leads individuals, families, and groups to more confidence in the ability to apply these life skills to their lives and relationships."

Our group first spent time meeting the horses in the field. We were then invited into the barn to try to move a horse around the corral without touching it. In our discussion that followed, I wondered to my group if I was bothering the horses during this exercise. The short training shed unexpected light on one of my tendencies to second guess myself that sometimes makes me feel a little uncertain in my social interactions with people. The awareness that animals can help us grow as humans is a concept that has many benefits. Perhaps the next time I find myself surrounded by curious four-hoofed creatures, I'll stick around a little longer.

12

MICE AREN'T NICE

I like to think of myself as brave. The day a mouse came unannounced into my house, however, almost did me in. It wasn't the first time one had taken a liking to my abode. The first incident happened a few years ago while I was entertaining an old friend in my living room. Kristie took a bite from a tasty snack I'd set out for her and sat up suddenly, looking toward the front door. "A mouse just walked in your house," she explained.

We sat the rest of the time with our feet up, discussing what I should do next as though we were exchanging recipes. She apologized for having to leave me alone with my visitor before heading out (a little too suddenly, in my opinion). I silently chided myself for not having hired a professional to install my storm door. Instead, another friend had obliged, and now it sat a full inch off the floor, the gleam of light escaping from the bottom enticing all manner of creatures to stop by on their evening strolls through the neighborhood. That day, it was a field mouse. Somehow I was able to coax it back out from the coat closet and into daylight the next morning.

The second mouse entered more stealthily. I saw signs of him in the kitchen, but convincing myself the black pellets scattered intermittently in a drawer were simply burned rice — only I hadn't cooked any rice — I proceeded on as if I were in some altered state of denial. Then I heard him rustling around one night. It sounded like he was unwrapping tiny Christmas presents in the pantry. I screamed in revulsion, frustration and helplessness. Then I called my sister and told her about it.

What to do? She suggested hiring an exterminator — but that cost money. I wanted to call a husband. Only, there is no husband yet. Sad and resigned, I decided this was going to be between me and the tiny rodent. I hoped he would leave on his own. For a couple more days, I saw and heard nothing. Then he was at it again. I reached for some Reese's Peanut Butter Cup Minis I had cached away, only to find he had beaten me to them. Indignant, I thought, "Oh-no-he-didn't!" It was bad enough he thought we had become chummy roommates overnight and wasn't paying rent. His overall behavior was just beyond disrespectful.

Don't get me wrong. The mouse and I had some things in common. We both loved hanging out where the food was, and we were especially delighted by peanut butter and chocolate blends. We both liked to travel and explore our surroundings. We both were messy eaters. We were both brownish. The list goes on. But he had crossed the line when he touched my chocolate and, despite our commonalities, I decided this mouse had to be executed.

I set a trap for him, using his weakness against him. I put cheese AND a Reese's candy inside, then I left the house for a few days. When I returned, lo and behold, he had fallen for it. I had caught my very first mouse. I screamed again with a mixture of trembling and triumph, then I called my sister back to tell her about my victory.

"Yay!" she exclaimed, the pride she felt for me spilling out of her voice. I felt powerful, in control and capable. Strangely, all these emotions arose from defeating a mouse.

I am woman. Hear me scream in terror, then roar.

13

ON PAIN AND ILLNESS

A brief sickness is an inconvenience — it means we probably won't get that project at work done on time after all, or we'll have to skip a few activities for the week and rest. But what if your ailment doesn't leave? What if the pain greets you the moment you awake and doesn't leave without medical intervention? What if your lost mobility prevents you from ever having the life you once lived?

That's called chronic illness, and it affects millions of people. A young woman we'll call Jaye recently told me her story. During a missions trip in 2006, she contracted a respiratory infection that took her voice for most of the trip. Her voice finally returned on the very last day, and once back in the United States, she began to recuperate. But then she fell ill again, losing her voice once more. This occurred several times before her voice finally disappeared altogether.

She went from doctor to doctor attempting to remedy the problem. She also was sent to speech and physical therapy, both of which were unsuccessful. In addition, she'd developed chronic fatigue, fibromyalgia, severe neck and back pain, fevers, an autonomic disorder, GI problems and seizures. Finally, she was sent to Emory Medical Center for more tests, speech therapy and treatment, "They were amazing. My voice is now a million times better," she said, though her voice might best be described as a coarse whisper.

It stands in contrast to the peppy and vibrant voice that is still on her phone, inviting one to leave a message. Doctors have told her that she might have a severe case of spasmodic dysphonia; they believe the original sickness caused her vocal cord muscles to tighten and spasm, causing a diminished ability to speak. Botox treatments have helped, and she reports, "I'm stubborn." Single and in her late 20s, she completed her counseling degree with the help of an understanding faculty, but her dream of doing therapy has been placed on hold. Working another job, she says, "My goal is 35 hours, but on a good week, it's usually between 25 and 30 hours." Sometimes, she has to take extended breaks, she said.

"I used to be super high energy, didn't need much sleep and was even training for a marathon," she said. "Pain robs you of so many things." One of the biggest issues facing those with chronic illnesses is the grief that follows the loss of your former life — one's abilities, outlook, even relationships change. Daily, one must fight to do the basic things, which can deplete energy, joy and optimism. For Jaye, her struggle has produced the unlikely fruit of what she describes as spiritual brokenness, a surrender that has surfaced in her conversations with God.

She has days when she feels closer to God than ever, then others that seem to be riddled with her own anger, sorrow and frustration. She has learned to long for God like never before, she says, and has developed a new appreciation for the perfection and hope of heaven. Humble and down-to-earth, Jaye is the epitome of honest struggle, strength and perseverance. "Where I come from, people love storms," she said. "I love the rain. I'm asking God to teach me to dance in the rain."

14

BUGGIES AND CHOCOLATE

*L*ancaster County, Pa. I imagined it to be a vast Eden-like place of soft rolling hills, white fluffy sheep and buggies. It is home to a large community of Amish, a unique group of Christians who fled Europe under persecution from both Protestants and Catholics and found refuge in the grasslands of America in the 1700s. Of mostly German descent, they still speak a dialect of the language among themselves and have preserved an austere and plain way of living that shruggs off the conveniences and so-called progress of modern life, attempting to remain separate from the many temptations of the world.

They don't drive cars or make use of electricity. Mostly farmers and small business owners, they use creative and practical measures to power their equipment and trade with the "English" — their non-Amish neighbors. I'd been fascinated by their culture since I'd first learned of them, so when I discovered that a conference I was attending in Pennsylvania was very near the community, I planned to visit.

In my reading, I stumbled upon a popular village named Intercourse that made me joke, "These people may not be as plain as we thought." I booked a tour bus and drove toward my destination. Of course, I got off track. When I discovered I was headed toward Hershey, I decided to pass through it first. I entered the village on

Chocolate Avenue, the wide grin on my face unmasking a sweet tooth or two.

A stranger had already pointed me toward The Hershey Story, where visitors could browse a museum, watch a documentary on chocolate and custom make a candy bar. Inside, I participated in the chocolate lab, where I learned about the varieties of cacao grown in several spots around the world. My respect lay with the Mayans, who understood the mysterious benefits of the cacao seed thousands of years ago and brewed it for special occasions — like for warriors going off to battle.

Our instructor gave us a tasting. I admired the sharp and bitter beginning of the Mexican chocolate and its cherry notes that emerged while going down. My lifelong passion for chocolate was only deepened through this cherished swallowing. I made my very own chocolate bar with sprinkles of hot pepper and cinnamon (just like the Mayans) and, after it was adequately hardened in its molding, tucked it into my purse to continue my journey.

I finally arrived in Lancaster and took a tour bus through the farmlands. I was thrilled to see the occasional buggy, apron-clad girls walking along the road barefoot and a peaceful church service going on in someone's backyard. It was like stepping back in time for an hour and a half. I almost forgot I was the lone passenger on a big bus, the absurdity swallowed up in fascination. I was surprised to see how many cars and houses of the English were scattered around, mixed in with Amish farms.

Upon my return to the outside, I stopped at a clothing store to browse and, feeling overwhelmed by the options, I thought of the simple life I had just left, where thoughts of what to wear are already decided by the community through hundreds of years of tradition. My tour guide and I had talked about the dating habits of the Amish (three years of official courting) and the importance of family and community.

He discussed the reality TV shows about the group, sharing which ones he believed to be completely fictitious. I respected the fact that, at 18, each Amish youth must make a personal choice on whether to remain in the community or leave for the outside world. Those who choose the latter must do so after tremendous soul-searching and bravery. The ones who remain enjoy the benefits of a peaceful and orderly world, generally more wholesome and predictable than that of the modern culture around them.

15

WOMEN WHO FIGHT FOR FREEDOM

Not all women want to stay home and guard the loot while men go off to war. Some want a piece of the action. Twenty-five- year-old Roberta (not her real name) was one such woman. Born in Japan to adventurous ex-pat parents, she spent part of her growing-up years in Germany and various parts of the United States. She ended up in military service, however, for one simple reason — it was a ticket to college.

"It's kind of funny. I was in high school and I wanted to go to college, but I couldn't afford it. I was told there was this small chance of winning a ROTC scholarship for school," she says. Roberta actually was awarded $85,000 toward her pursuit of higher education. There was just one catch. She had to enlist.

After completing basic training, she came home and began school at a nearby military college. Toward the end of her first year, she was deployed to Iraq. The scholarship should have prevented this and, had certain people come to her defense, she might have been able to remain at school. For unknown reasons this did not happen, and Roberta found herself headed for war.

"I wasn't scared by any means," she remembers. She figured once she did her year abroad, she'd be right back at school, finishing up her goals. The challenges she faced as a military woman in Iraq were complex. Often, she had to travel with at least two other females or one other male. This was not just for her protection from the enemy but also from her fellow comrades.

"Harassment didn't happen in our unit, but it did in other units. It got old quick, so I'd have to put [certain males] in their place. There were times it got pretty bad … They would try to take advantage of you … It takes a lot to unnerve me, but some females were really scared about it. 'I double dog dare you to put your hands on me,' that was my attitude."

Assaults against service members reached 26,000 in 2012, according to The Associated Press, though the military has been actively working to reduce these numbers and bring justice to victims. Roberta feels that many of the women who enlist may do so because they like the idea of secure employment, others seek self-confidence or are trying to escape from something back home.

Roberta soon settled into life in Iraq.

"Iraq was hot, super stressful, long days, not a lot of sleep. I'd work a 14-hour shift and come back to my trailer and lie down. Five minutes later [an alarm would sound], and I'd have to put my uniform and gear back on and walk a half mile to the command center to await instructions." To this day, Roberta can't stand the smell of Monster energy drinks because she drank so many of them to stay awake. Returning to life back in the States also can be a challenge. For one, she doesn't always fit in with non-military women.

"They don't think the same way or have the same outlook. I'm always aware of my surroundings. I know how to have a good time, but even then I know what's going on around me at all times. The women here aren't as confident as women I'm used to being around [in the military]."

Women suffer from post-traumatic stress just as men do. Though most people who encounter service members in uniform are polite and even congratulatory, Roberta has met a detractor or two. One such man heckled her in an airport, tried to stop her from walking away and spat at her. What followed was reported back to Roberta, because she blacked out.

"They said I screamed and punched him, then went over a seat with him. He went to the hospital, and I almost went to jail." Despite these types of episodes, Roberta is glad she enlisted. She remembers the camaraderie of her unit, how they looked out for each other, put each other's needs before their own.

"I can't imagine who I'd be if I hadn't joined," she says.

16

FAMILY HISTORY

When I think of family reunions, my mind conjures images of sitting in the summer heat at a picnic, swatting flies and hugging the necks of sweet kinfolk. The first and last full reunion I attended was so long ago I think I must have been in elementary school. I blame my aunt for my participation in our most recent family reunion, held earlier this month.

She told a cousin in Huntsville, Ala., that I should help represent one of our ancestors in a speech during the family dinner. I was asked to wear a long skirt and white-collar shirt and to pull my hair into a bun, typical of late 1800s attire. Intrigued, I agreed to the presentation, thinking, "Hmm, sounds interesting." I wanted to see what might transpire.

My maternal side of the family is originally from the Huntsville area, though now they are spread out coast to coast. My aunt and mother joined me and away we sped to Alabama for an evening with our large extended family. It turned out that about 18 of us would be presenting that night. Our theme was "Connecting the Past, Visualizing the Future."

The first woman who presented, apparently a very distant cousin of ours, did so with the flair of a professional actress. Dressed in slave clothes, she rendered a dramatic speech about being "Lucy," whom I discovered was my great-great-great grandmother. She was born a slave and bore a son named Samuel Arnett. Arnett married a woman named Louisa, and together they bore 15 children.

I represented the first of these offspring, also named Lucy after her grandmother. This Lucy was the mother of my grandmother. Like my grandmother, she was known for cooking delicious pound cakes and salmon croquettes. I learned that the family I had previously only known as "my mother's side" complete with its uncles, aunts and cousins, was called the "Lucy Line" in the big picture of family. Each of the lines was announced and asked to stand at the dinner.

As the evening wore on and each person depicted an ancestor with creativity and personal nuance, I sat back, watching and listening in amazement. Here was my love for story, theater, public speaking, and oral interpretation. I could see the same traits displayed in the playfulness and energy of the all the participants. My mother had excitedly shown me a book of pictures of the family that I had only glanced at before. Now I more fully understood the power and wonder of knowing your roots as I heard the anecdotes and brief histories of these blood relations I had never known about previously. They all came alive for me that night.

Our late cousin, Pat Lauderdale, was the beloved woman who had pulled the family stories together. She'd studied the family tree during her doctoral work, and then wrote as much of the history as she could. She then began organizing our reunions, asking others to spread the word and gather as much history and pictures as they could to be compiled and made into a family history book. Having just passed away a year ago, we honored her at the banquet, for without her, we would not have such a treasure chest of knowledge today. That said, I plan to be in full attendance at the next reunion, hopefully with a host of "Lucy Line" cousins, aunts and uncles in tow.

17

ANIMAL BULLIES

Animals are wonderful. Some can fly, others change colors, run fast or go months without eating. It's as if they have their own super powers. The most intelligent ones can be trained to do acrobatics, dance and perform other amazing feats. When I was a child, my family always had dogs and chickens, but the only pets I've taken care of as an adult were fish, and I didn't do so well with them. They seemed to always be getting a disease, or having their bowls accidentally turned over, causing them to flop on the floor and, of course, later getting another disease and having to be flushed down the toilet.

That aside, I've still been fascinated by interesting living creatures. Recently, however, I've had to face some unpleasant truths about some of my favorite animals and their lifestyles. For the longest time, I've wanted a pet miniature pig. I even had a screen saver on my work computer of an adorable black-and-white micro mini pig with hot-pink painted toes and colorful beads around her neck.

She was my inspiration, and the only reason I didn't order her from the Internet was that she cost over $800. Instead, I watched fun videos about mini pigs swimming, learning to climb stairs and oink around the houses of their delighted owners. And then I learned a startling possibility. Though these pigs start out very mini, according to how much they eat and their general genetics, they can still grow to about 80 pounds. Now that's miniature compared to large hogs that can tip the scales at over 500 pounds, but still. At 80 pounds, that's a hard creature to curl up to at night. I've since dropped the idea and moved on to exotic goats.

And then there was the disturbing information about dolphins. I have always loved them for being so smart, free spirited and always wearing a smile. But I've recently learned that they can be aggressive toward smaller porpoises, sometimes tossing them around in the water and biting them for the fun of it. In more extreme cases, they have been known to kill these genetic cousins for no reason at all. They have also been observed kidnapping and violating female dolphins. I've always wanted to swim with dolphins, but now I'm concerned the bullies of the species may try to drown me.

My last "wild kingdom" story occurred on my front porch last week. Because I love hanging ferns, I'm used to birds building nests in them. I don't always see eggs or baby birds, and sometimes I pluck the nests out before they can lay. (I'm no saint). But this year each fern held several eggs each in their nests. They hatched at around the same time. I proudly showed off my babies to my visitors. One woman almost cried when the mama and daddy birds showed up to feed their chirping offspring while we sat chatting. Well, the very next day I got up and went to the window to observe. Immediately I could see that one fern was pressed down on one side. I knew something was wrong. I went out to look. Sure enough, all the birds were gone, the nest had been tossed aside, and a couple of feathers lay on the ground below. I was genuinely sad that they had apparently been eaten by a cat (according to my brother) or an owl (my father's hypothesis).

At this point, I think I'll just focus on gardening.

18

LET'S RIDE

I have scars on each knee that I've sported most of my life. Here's the back story:

Picture this, East Ridge (a neighborhood on the southeast corner of Chattanooga) in the early '80s. I am feeling fearless and invincible on what I know now was just a dinky little bike. At the time I must have thought it was a Harley. I am riding down the hill in front of our house, the first house I remember, with the wind in my face and exhilaration egging me on from behind.

After a few breathless downward treks, I decide to intensify the experience. This time, in the middle of the ride, I swing my feet up onto the handlebars and lift my hands upward to the sky. Ahh, for a few seconds it was amazing.

The next thing I remember though is the sickening sensation of falling, the crunch of the bike against the gravel, the scraping of skin, the sound of my own screaming, blood running down my legs and, for the rest of my life, scars.

Age and distraction eventually caused me to focus on other things besides daredevil bike rides. Last week, however, I bought a new bicycle for exercise. I decided on a man's bike only because the handlebars were higher on one particular model and I thought I could handle it, being an above-average woman (in size, that is.) After I purchased it online, it arrived. My neighbor, a cyclist, put it together for me.

It was a little too tall at first, but he made it work by lowering the seat as far down as he could make it go. After that, we were off for my first ride. I was wondering how aerobic cycling would be because, when I was younger, I could bike for hours. Well, I was about to find out how much I had aged.

We crossed the street out of our neighborhood and started up a slight incline. Halfway up, I was hyperventilating and so nauseous I had no choice but to stop and put my head down on the handle bars, sucking in breaths for dear life. My neighbor tried to encourage me onward, but I told him in no uncertain terms it wasn't happening that day. Why did he take us away from our neighborhood and onto a hill? I wondered with mild indignation. With a background in the military, I should have known he'd push me to my limits.

I tried to regain my composure, feeling lightheaded and close to fainting. Wow. What a difference a few decades and a couple of pounds make (OK, well maybe more than a couple.) As soon as the nausea subsided, I turned my bike around and coasted back down the small hill. The wind in my face was not nearly as exhilarating as that ride I took many years ago, but it was certainly welcome. It meant I didn't have to pedal for a few seconds.

When we arrived back at my house this time, I felt nervous about stopping the bike. I squeezed the brakes a little too hard and felt the back tire lift up and plop down again, landing safely but humorously on the sidewalk. My front tire was still on the road. I laughed at what this must have looked like from behind while my neighbor demonstrated the correct way to brake and dismount.

I had faced my demise yet again and overcome. All in all, it was a great ride.

19

CAKE CLASS CATASTROPHE

I'm usually the one who brings the potato chips to potlucks. I wouldn't describe myself as the least domestic of women. During the dark ages of my middle-school years, my sister and I discovered an amazing recipe for chewy, buttery oatmeal cookies that adults were willing to purchase from us. We spent our weekends baking and perfecting their texture and taste until we actually created a pretty consistent demand for our product.

After college, when I tired of eating made-up soup concoctions, ramen noodles and bland veggies, I cut out beautiful food pictures from magazines and began to try out tasty recipes. I had a wonderful roommate who taught me how to set up a flavor bouquet for sautéing with peppers, garlic and onions, and another who actually showed me how to clean, skin, and cut up a squid, then batter and fry it into delicious calamari rings. These were exciting times in food.

These days, I am expanding my baking skills. I've dreamed of presenting beautiful desserts to others at holiday times or after a delicious dinner at my house. The details of baking seemed more difficult to teach one's self than cooking. I don't remember who first told me about them, but when I heard about Wilton cake-decorating classes offered at a local crafts store, I knew I had to try.

It was a welcome change from my regular world. After a hectic week, I could end each Friday for a month by escaping into a room of individuals making sugared roses pushed daintily out of bags of colored icing. I could enjoy creating sweet cupcakes and sumptuous cakes that would ease my mind and stir my creative juices, allowing me to gently unwind from the week. Plus, I'd be able to show off my skills to others. At least that's what I thought, anyway.

Turns out, cake decorating is not as easy as it looks. It takes patience, preparation, imagination and organization. I found I was an eager yet lazy student. I looked forward to classes but scrambled at the last minute to gather all my tools. Inevitably, I never got everything done in time. My saving grace was my diligent and generous coworker who'd agreed to take the class with me. Armed with a background in elementary education, coupled with years of engaging children in counseling offices and church groups, she knew how to prepare for the details. She read the instructions carefully, completed her homework and appeared in class with her homemade icings in nicely mixed colors, neat cakes that had been correctly pressed down and a stiff apron ready for the show.

Me? I borrowed items from her. My cake arrived still warm in the pan from a frantic baking right before class. My cupcakes were ugly. The icing was store bought. My nerves were frayed. Feeling like the kid in class who is always a step behind and can't figure out why, the teacher casually blessed my icing flowers with a simple, "Pretty" as she walked slowly around the class inspecting our efforts. I glowed with pride.

Sometimes in life you have to be satisfied with the little achievements. I'll never be a renowned cake decorator, but perhaps I'll feel the satisfaction of being a little above average among regular folk. At least that's what I'd like to think. Work with me, people …

20

LAUGH AWAY YOUR CARES

The other night I came home from work, curled up in bed with my laptop computer and watched brief comedy episodes for over an hour. It had been a long day at work, and I was dog tired. I thought briefly of the productive things I should have tackled that evening. But in my haze of passivity, all I really wanted to do was laugh and enjoy mindless entertainment. That's what happened. I smiled, I giggled. I threw my head back at ironic moments, guffawed at silly stories, and for one brief moment, screamed out my mirthful surprise.

By the end of the evening, I felt more energetic, less stressed and actually happier than at its beginning. I marveled again at the effect that smiling, laughing and relaxing has on us humans. One of my favorite memories of childhood is my mom sitting in front of the television and laughing nonstop for 30 minutes as she watched episodes of "America's Funniest Home Videos." It put the whole family in a good mood. We'd come and sit with her from time to time just to watch her laugh and to join in at especially good moments.

We've all heard that laughter is the best medicine. The effects of laughter on our bodies are immense. Laughing boosts our immune system, relieves pain, relaxes muscles, strengthens the heart, helps us refresh ourselves and releases toxins. It increases our oxygen levels and thereby helps with blood circulation. It helps us bond with others, brings balance to our daily lives by allowing us to be in the moment, decreases depression and anxiety, attracts others to us, and can dramatically alter our perspective on life in a matter of minutes.

Today, people hold seminars in which you learn to laugh. There is even laughter yoga. Its benefits are used to help the elderly cope, heal cancer patients and even offset pain after surgery. We are all born with great senses of humor, but some of us seem to lose it along the way. The pressures of life can steer us toward a mentality of heaviness or disappointment. The art of laughing is needed more than ever in times of sadness, high anxiety and fear.

We literally must choose laughter, as I did the other night when I could have been doing more serious things. It turned out that those things still needed to get done, but tackling them later became easier once I'd blown off a little steam in the laughing room of life.

Want to bring more laughter into your life? Try these techniques:

- Hang out with children. They generally live to laugh and play and will look for humor in everyday situations.
- One writer suggests moving toward laughter when you hear it nearby and asking, "What's funny?" Most people enjoy sharing humor with others.
- Learn to tell jokes and enjoy a good ribbing now and then. As a child, I was amazed that my father could get total strangers to warm up to him by just telling them funny stories and boldly teasing them.
- Watch comedy, read comedy, listen to comedy.
- Of course, remember to laugh at yourself more than at other people.

Now, let me tell you a funny story...

PART III
HOLIDAYS

"No holidays, no country."
— Toba Beta

21

LIGHT

Lights are twinkling in my fireplace, across its mantel and atop my kitchen cabinets. Lights are blinking outside on houses, in store windows and dazzling the streets. These stunning orbs of radiance signal that the holidays are here. Light is essential to almost all celebrations during this season. Not big, bright lights that overwhelm the senses but lights that shine in the middle of the dark. Lights during the winter solstice remind us that in the middle of the season's dim coldness, light and life will come again.

Christmas is celebrated to remind us that the Light of the World has penetrated our spiritual blindness and revealed holy truth to us. The Advent season that leads up to the actual holiday encourages the lighting of candles and a specific meditation each day.

Kwanzaa, the African-American holiday beginning the day after Christmas, also has to do with lights, which reveal core values in East African language. Hanukkah lights remind the Jews of the supply of oil, only enough for a day, that miraculously lasted eight days. The lighting of the menorah is done as an aid to reflecting on the victory they had hundreds of years ago to regain control over and to rededicate the temple, reinstitute their religious traditions and to overcome the powers that existed at that time.

Light shines in darkness this season, but the holidays remain dark to many people. Some have lost loved ones and miss them terribly.

Others' homes or treasured possessions have been ripped from them through natural disaster, economic tidal waves or relational war. A friend and I watched the incredibly well-written and performed holiday movie musical "Black Nativity" over Thanksgiving weekend. After singing and dancing in the theater along with the on-screen cast, we reflected on its powerfully redemptive themes over dinner afterward. Aren't we all like these characters, we asked ourselves, caught up in our own pain until someone reveals a new side to our often bitter and dismal stories, offering us a chance to be free.

The light shines in darkness, bringing hope, then joy. Light has many definitions: illumination or brightness, to ignite something, to be playful and entertaining, cheerful, easy, soft and even elegant. Oh to be light, to see light, to have light shining in our heaviness, our despair and our dealings with death. This is the hope of the holidays, and we might miss it if we don't take the time to pause and reflect.

I was invited to a Hanukkah celebration at a Messianic Jewish congregation on Saturday. There, the restful colors of blue and white greeted my eyes upon entering, the menorah candlestick faced the congregation and drew my attention, the pageantry of the Torah scroll unfolding helped me understand the need for reverence and awe. The women dancing around the congregation brought joy to me, the singing throughout calmed, the power of spontaneous prayers at the close moved my soul.

What joy of togetherness, of remembering, of connecting to the past and understanding how it links to the now. When we transcend our circumstances, our seeming dead-ends and last chances through the rituals of remembering, we reclaim the prizes that give meaning and beauty to life. We look back at our broken pathways, and we see something different. This helps us move forward again, to see a new life ahead. And this is imperative to living in joy. We have heard that joy has nothing to do with what has happened but everything to do with the spin we put on what happened. In order to have joy, we must find the others also seeking it, link with them, receive and give love to each other, remember together, celebrate together and stay in the Light together.

22

A NEW YEAR'S DETOX

While shopping at a health food store the other day, a friend and I stumbled upon a section that featured cleanses and detoxes. My friend wanted to try one as a way to help jump-start her healthy-living goals for the New Year. I told her I'd done more than one in my years, and though I wasn't sure if it had had lasting effects, she should give it a whirl. Many people seemed to really benefit from them.

Some of us surely need a cleanse this year, but more of the emotional kind. If you're like me, just because the clock struck midnight on New Year's morning, life didn't automatically reset itself. We still have some of the same struggles from the past, wishes yet to be fulfilled, dreams still to be pursued. What we may need to really turn the corner of change, however, is to let go of some old things in order to make room for the newness a new year so monumentally symbolizes.

Here are a few ideas:

Cleanse yourself of fear that paralyzes. Fear is often the silent stumbling block that prevents us from taking much needed risks. There are risks that really don't cost much. We are afraid of this type only because we simply dislike the possibility of failing. The fear of failure, when allowed to fester and grow, can be a deterrent to success. Not trying will cost you more frustration, feelings of persecution and feelings of failure anyway. You may as well push this block to the side and see what happens. You can be proud of yourself for that small step of progress.

Cleanse yourself of mental and physical clutter, which promotes anxiety. Pace yourself for success. Doing one thing a day will help you accomplish seven things by the end of just one week. Cleanse yourself of toxic people in your inner circle with an energy of positive regard. I had a talk with a woman the other day about just such a relationship. Even when she attempted kindness with this person, it was used against her, often harshly. She had come to the logical conclusion that distance was the only safe stance, but she took her position with freedom and thoughtful resignation, not pain or anger. She would have continued in kindness had it been safe for her, but it wasn't. It's important to know who should be close to us and who should not, but doing so with negative energy only keeps the poison in. We must learn to let them go in peace and goodwill.

Cleanse yourself of a lifestyle you can no longer manage. When I was younger, I loved the feeling of constant motion. I traveled, spent time with friends, studied, exercised and worked with gusto. As I've gotten up in years, though, I've realized I need much more quiet times to feel sane. It's a slightly different life, but one I can better handle.

Cleanse yourself of excuses. Oh, how I hate this cleanse. I really love my excuses. They help me wriggle out of responsibility for so many things. But if I am to make progress, I've got to change my language of explaining why so many things haven't worked, can't work, will never work, to a solution-focused curiosity about what needs to occur to create synergistic change.

Happy detoxing!

23

VALENTINE'S DAY

Happy Love Day! I know, I know. Some people quietly endure this day of hearts. It makes them mad or sad if they have no Special Someone to enjoy it with. Or their Special Someone is less than appealing lately. Others can't stomach the pressure of one more jewelry commercial showing "oohy gooey" in love people surprised by rings and necklaces, and resist the societal expectation to show love in a materialistic way.

Despite the various perspectives out there, I am strangely drawn to Valentine's Day. For all those who disdain a day like today, perhaps I can inspire you to take a second look. Let's spend the next few minutes celebrating it together. Come into this space, imagine it strewn with rose petals, see the welcoming candle, hear the restful music, and notice the suspended, floating poetry. In other words, will you be my Valentine? Just give it a try ...

A poem came across my email a few days ago. It was written by a popular 13th century Persian poet named Jalaluddin Rumi. The verse makes a deep impact:

"Your task is not to seek love, but merely to seek and find all the barriers within yourself that you have built against it." If you're like me, the idea of not seeking love feels counterintuitive. Most of us love to find love but are often disappointed because, true to what Rumi perceives, we are unaware that when we struggle, the barriers we face to finding love in sustainable ways are most often hidden deep within ourselves.

The type of poetry Rumi wrote was considered ecstatic love poetry, meant to help a person journey from physical ideals to a much deeper, divine level of understanding. Reflecting, one assumes that, once we remove our barriers, love may come flooding in. That would mean that love is all around us. Perhaps the barrier of fear keeps it from some of us, or self-protection, or disappointing memories and negative expectations. Perhaps these types of internal edifices blind us in some way, keeping us separated from what we really want in life — in essence, to feel useful, connected and happy.

Of course, this love is not necessarily romantic. Please sample the delicious chocolates I'm offering you now in our imaginary space and think on this. The Greeks believed there were four types of love: *eros* (romantic, sensual love), *philia* (brotherly, friendship love), *storge* (instinctual, parental love) and *agape* (perfect, unconditional love.) If we take inventory of our lives, we can become aware that sometimes our perceived external blockages to having what we want can be removed by going inside.

For example, I desire to experience storge love in the experience of being a parent, but I have no children. In my zeal, I have at times tried to parent other adults. This usually ends disastrously. Other times I have yielded to anxiety over this lack. Finally, I have entertained creative, out-of-the-box ways to manifest this type of love — through mentoring, teaching, playfully noticing and encouraging the young. From this I learned that even literal blockages can have secret passageways around them. One can find other unique ways to overcome an obstacle to a certain type of love.

Now sip some of this refreshing beverage: Love is good. Celebrating it is wonderful. Our creative minds help us move past stuck places and frustrating emotions. Sometimes we need wise guides, such as insightful friends, good writing, new ideas. Rest awhile on this soft pillow of imagination. When you are ready, enjoy the rest of your day, sharing it with others… in love.

24

BLACK HISTORY HAS A SOUNDTRACK

In the days when slaves dotted the cotton fields of the South, they often passed the time and expressed their thoughts and emotions through extemporaneous musical shouts and rambles called "field hollers." These musical forms gave way to work songs, which were repeated by others often in a "call and response" style. Historians describe the "call and response" as a spontaneous and rhythmic verbal, and even nonverbal, interaction between a speaker and listener who responds to what's being said or sung. Some of these early music forms are considered to be the precursors of the blues.

Black music history evolved along with the history and evolution of the people. During slavery, spirituals were often sung, some giving hints of how to escape to freedom using language from the Bible. For example, "crossing the River Jordan" had a dual meaning. It referred to entering paradise after death and also obtaining freedom from slavery by escaping to the North. People sang what became known as freedom songs during the Civil Rights movement. Spiritual music, often in the form of gospel, also influenced soul and R&B genres.

Black music, which has had a major impact on what would become known as American music in general, is characterized by improvisation, or simply being in the moment, responding to one's own emotions through song. Many songs which became more soul in nature make use of what are called blue notes, or flat notes sung just below a more mainstream note. In jazz and ragtime examples, we see the use of syncopation, a deviation from the main tune, adding in extra notes and arrangements.

There are some historical musical greats that receive very little press today. One of these is Thomas Wiggins, also called Thomas Bethune. Though what we would call autistic today and blind, he was a musical prodigy with an almost magical talent. Historians tell us he was born a slave in 1849 and along with his parents was sold to a Georgia lawyer named Neil Bethune as an infant.

He could pick out tunes on a piano and reproduce them by the time he was 4. He had his first concert at age 8. He could recite a poem or perform a piece of music after hearing it only one time. His owner began hiring him out as a musician and published some of his songs. Blind Tom, as he was called, eventually played the works of Bach, Chopin, Liszt, Beethoven and Thalberg. He traveled and performed at concerts in the 1800s, and it was said that he brought in revenue of about $50,000 a year, eventually making his representatives and owners a fortune. He was able to play two different songs at the same time and sing a third. He could also mimic nature and animal sounds and repeat whole conversations verbatim.

Another historical great was Florence Beatrice Smith Price, who was the first black female composer of symphonic music. Born in 1887 to professional and educated parents, her mother taught her to play the piano at a young age; she later studied music formally. Her "Symphony in E minor" was played by the Chicago Symphony Orchestra. She went on to write chamber music, classical music, spirituals and vocal works. She was active in the New Negro Arts Movement and wrote more than 300 musical works. She often used the pseudonym Veejay, and even wrote music for silent movies.

Closer to our time, the Funky Four Plus One More is a rap group that made music history by having the first female rapper. They were signed to a record label, Enjoy Records, in 1979. The Funky Four Plus One More was also the first rap group to ever perform on live national television, appearing on the hit sketch comedy show "Saturday Night Live" on Valentine's Day in 1981.

These musical greats, little known today, have helped shape the vast culture and exciting history of a musical form that continues to evolve and influence the music of the world.

25

MOTHER'S DAY

On a fun family trip to Disney World, a friend told me she'd met two amazing little girls one night as they exited an elevator heading for dinner. They were dolled up in beautiful spring dresses and accompanied by their parents. As they energetically conversed with her in fresh, sprightly Welsh accents, my friend was delighted by their open, friendly style and energy. As they parted to leave, their mother asked them, "Girls, what do you say to the lady?" They turned to my friend and said in unison, "You look amazing!"

"And what else?" their mother gently prodded. Looking up at my friend again, they said with zest, "Invest in yourself!" And pranced off happily to dinner. My friend was stunned. Tears sprang to her eyes. The encounter with these lovely young girls left her breathless and aware of something she had needed desperately. She, who had struggled for so long with her own value and self-worth, had come face to face with two sisters who would probably never have that struggle. They were being taught to love themselves, to celebrate themselves and to grace others with words of encouragement and affirmation.

Their mother, no doubt standing proudly behind them, had very craftily taught her daughters to reenact this scene over and over with the strangers they came in contact with, wisely knowing their unique power as children, and the gift and reinforcement it would be to them to see the wonderful impact of their own words on others.

Their mother was much more than a good mother. She was a grand, amazing, thoughtful, and actively engaged mother. She had thought through the messages her daughters should receive and taught them to give those same messages to others generously.

I'm encouraged by the many great mothers I know in this world. These mothers love their children fiercely, protect them, teach them, push them. They are priceless. These mothers are those who teach their children how to see themselves accurately and then to reflect that beauty outward, like the mother just mentioned.

They are unafraid to set high standards and model them, like the mother I know who doesn't allow her daughter to have opposite sex visitors in the house when she's not there, even though her daughter is over 18 years old now. The daughter and her boyfriend often sit on her porch talking, waiting respectfully for her to come home. The admiration her children have for her is evident.

There are great mothers who have willingly fought for their own emotional healing in order to better care for their children and give them the love they did not receive when they were growing up. Others have sacrificed time, dreams, and comfort to place their children in situations they felt were best for them. Others have stood by offspring who have deeply disappointed them and fallen short of the hopes they passionately held for them at their earliest moments, continuing to believe in them and urge them forward with enduring love.

Great mothers also come in the form of neighbors who look out for the children on their block, educators who continue to pour into the young lives that sit before them every day, foster parents who look after the little ones others were unable to, and strangers who sow kind words into the ears of those who will listen. To all these mothers, including my own great mother, I say thank you and Happy Mother's Day.

26

FATHER'S DAY

Father's Day has come and gone, but I still can't stop thinking about dads. My father enjoyed engaging us children. I still remember jumping in the car with him after basketball practice one day in middle school, asking him to drop off a friend.

"Sure," he said, and proceeded to talk easily about the day while he drove. My friend stepped out of the car later, her jaw close to the ground.

"I can't believe your dad talks to you like that!" she said in disbelief.

I was confused. "Like what?" I wondered. She later explained that her dad hardly ever talked to his family. Having a verbally connected father has shaped me in countless ways. For one, I put as much of a premium on Father's Day as Mother's Day. I've noticed this is not the norm. Some people told me they sent texts to their dads. Others didn't do much at all.

On Monday, I listened to radio personalities joke about the disappointments some fathers endured on their special day, something rarely heard on Mother's Day. It's no secret the world is putting less value on the presence and power of the father. Worse, many men themselves don't know how important they are to their children.

In 2006, interviewer Nancy Madsen asked former pro-football player Bill Glass what he thought was the country's biggest problem. He answered, "The lack of the father's blessing. The FBI studied the

17 kids that have shot their classmates in little towns like Paducah, Ky.; Pearl, Miss.; and Littleton, Colo. All 17 shooters had one thing in common. They had a father problem. I see it so much; it's just unbelievable. There's something about it when a man doesn't get along with his father. It makes him mean; it makes him dangerous; it makes him angry."

After years of working in the nation's prisons and detention centers, Glass said he has noticed that no other issue seems to be the most consistent with the inmates. He said that his father would kiss him goodnight and tell him what a good boy he was. He himself has hugged and kissed his own 250-pound boys on numerous occasions.

On Father's Day, my own daddy gave me and my siblings one of the most amazing gifts I have ever received: a written blessing. He spoke to us about our character, what he sees for our future, the hopes and dreams he has for us. The moment he read mine, I felt totally caught off guard with wonder and gratitude. I felt as though I had just been knighted and should've been bowing humbly before a king.

But even a father not so eloquent can bless his child. A simple, "I really like you, kid," will do fine. Bill Glass went on to say that when he "… grabbed that eldest son of mine recently and said, 'I love you, I bless you, I think you're terrific, and I'm so glad you're mine," his shoulders began to shake and his eyes filled with tears, as he said, 'Dad, I really needed that.'" That's the power of a father's positive words and heart toward his children.

27

A RELUCTANT THANKSGIVING

Sometimes it is difficult to give thanks. When life has been so good for so long that pain is shocking. When blessings have rained down so softly, with little fanfare, that ease is normal. When the big fluffy blanket is pulled away during a cool night, while you are sleeping in a quiet neighborhood, with food in the refrigerator, with clothes in the closet -- sometimes, it is difficult to give thanks.

When life is tough, though, gratitude is sometimes easier. This year, I have endured a broken engagement, a broken car, a broken heart. I felt I was suffering, and to be sure, there was some truth to that. But in the midst of it was the discovery that the world I had reluctantly returned to was actually my oasis in the desert. Surrounded by family and friends, I was buffered from deeper pain. The basic blessings of my life became my focus. I read a column weeks ago that briefly chronicled the life of a Muslim prostitute. She said wryly, "Some would say I am lucky." She knew that what she had, though meager, was *all* that she had. Now that's perspective.

When I was in college, many miles away from home, I once went almost three weeks eating only two meals a day. I wanted to conserve money to help fund an international travel trip. I quit relishing the memory of sacrifice when I read about the families in central Africa who were eating every other day in order to conserve food during wartime and famine. My sacrifice became small in my own eyes, reduced to a sentimental gesture.

The traditional prayers of the black church are filled with simple statements such as, "Thank you Lord that I woke up in my right mind, that I have eyes to see, a voice to sing your praises " What must it be like to be so emptied out that the only thing you can sing about is being alive? There are folk songs that tell the stories of men with no shoes who thank God for feet. How freeing to be reduced to such basics that our eyes become transformed and we see what life is really made of.

It is wonderful when we strip it all away -- mutual fund losses, competition with our co-workers, the overtime we need at work to pay off consumer bills, the little time we have for friends and family. If we peel back the unnecessary layers of our lives, we find that the simplicity is refreshing. When we have less to worry about, plan for, escape from, wallow in, we find that we have at least one or two things to be ecstatic about.

On this holiday weekend, I am thankful that God loves me. I am thankful that I have a wonderful family, incredible friends and a soft bed to sleep in. The pilgrims offered simple prayers of thanks. They were thankful that they had stepped onto dry ground, tilled the land, created places to sleep. They were glad that they were together. Their journey had been difficult. Had they not left and lost loved ones? I had almost forgotten that the word for pilgrim means "wayfarer, journeyer." Are we not all pilgrims on our journey through this world? Have we not all come from a mighty, mighty long way? May we not be so shocked by occasional misery that we forget that occasional misery is an incredible blessing.

Let us not forget to be grateful that trouble does not last always, that there is a balm in Gilead, that joy comes in the morning. Let us remember that our journey has been splendid indeed. After all, we are alive.

28

GIVING THANKS AT THE FAMILY HEARTH

A friend recently told me that the Thanksgiving table was truly a symbol of the ideal family, something we all need and long for, but don't always experience. We discussed how the warmth that the table uniquely brings is related to the idea of a family hearth. The original hearth was the base of the fireplace that warmed the whole house. It became a symbol of the heart of family life. It was where we all gathered to take in warmth, eat, talk, laugh, and enjoy life together. Today, the kitchen seems to be the new hearth, with the table as its center. But simply gathering together creates its own hearth.

I once held a Giving Thanks gathering in which people were asked to tell an encouraging story, sing a song, read a poem, etc. that told a personal story of gratefulness. One woman told of surviving 20 months of unemployment and illness, citing several miraculous occurrences along the way. Another told of several surgeries, operations that should have left her with far less mobility than she actually has. She was grateful for her activity levels and health. Others closed their eyes and sang their hearts out. One woman who after giving birth to a beautiful daughter, wrote in her journal about how happy she was although she was still suffering some complex physical consequences of the delivery and could not walk for weeks.

The stories of thanksgiving all had some level of suffering at-
tached to them. They chose to give thanks in the midst of the struggle, to have faith, to keep believing, to do what needed to be done,
and in the end they were rewarded.

They had somehow found a spiritual hearth, a place to focus
what little warmth could be found in their chilly circumstances. They
chose to sit close and appreciate what it brought to them.

So this Thanksgiving, let's forget about someone else's ideal for a
wonderful holiday, and let's celebrate whatever small glowing ember
we can find in the midst of a small fire. Perhaps this time can be a
doorway to new ways to appreciate family, friends, and life. Let this
hearth be our symbolic place where we find comfort in all that is less
than ideal, forgetting the rest for just a little while.

29

CHRISTMAS EVE

Hey, come on in. It's Christmas Eve, and whether you're with family today, alone or not celebrating, I'd like to invite you to this unique gathering of friends, family and strangers happening right here on this page. As I write and as you read, I'd like us to reflect on the hope, the joy and the expectation that this day represents.

Earlier this week, on the first day of winter, I awoke to a landscape white with frost. The blue-purple pansies I'd just planted had frozen solid. My car was an icebox that I scraped three times before I could see through the windshield. Frustrated and cold, I was cranky as I began my day. By noon, however, the air was so warm I resented my thermal leggings. I returned home to find that my pansies had shed their frigid layers and had popped up with flair. My car was cozy again. That day that began as cold, uncomfortable, and harsh had gradually returned to normal.

This reminds me of how things in life can come full circle — like the friendship I reconciled in July. We first met 10 years ago in Atlanta, when both of us were struggling to find jobs and make sense of life after graduate school.

Tensions in our lives were high, and one day we had an argument. I said some insensitive things to my friend, and we eventually parted ways. As the years passed, I sometimes thought of her and my misguided temper, and wished I could make things right.

I finally located her on the Internet and contacted her. We began the tentative journey of repairing an old relationship. This week, I received a gorgeous gift from her in the mail. The card was a touching reminder of the beauty of rekindled friendship, and how life can surprise us by reconnecting loose ends. I trust you've tied some loose ends of your own this year. Sometimes, however, things don't tie up so neatly, and we still must press on.

On Christmas Eve at the family house, Daddy will usually read the Christmas story from the gospel of Luke. Last year, he gave a one-man play that caused the grandkids to squeal in delight. On Christmas mornings, Mama often bakes sweet bread that makes the morning air sing with delicious odors. Growing up, she sometimes asked us kids to give our siblings a non-tangible gift, such as an act of service or a gift of words. These are the traditions that deepen the meaning of the season.

This year, my six nieces and nephews won't be home for the holidays; and that means there'll be no running, screaming, high-pitched giggling, gingerbread houses only a grandmother would consider beautiful, spontaneous dances, impromptu theater productions, forts in the bedrooms, or fingers in the cake batter bowl. I will sorely miss them. Have you ever had a Christmas that was going to be really different than the ones before?

Sometimes you just have to take the wonderful things in life along with the imperfections, sort of like the false eyelashes I wore for a few weeks this summer. They were beautiful on me (my co-worker told me so) but when the removal glue got in my eyes and burned them so much I thought I'd go blind, I was reminded that beauty, like love, and even joy, sometimes requires a sacrifice. We've all had to make them.

Regardless of what tomorrow brings, I'm sure it will be good. Who knows, I may just love this unique Christmas. It may be one of the best I've ever had. Let's celebrate that in the most unlikely of moments, we can laugh. In the deadest times, life can spring forth again. In darkness, a light has dawned.

30

PEACE AND SURPRISES

The holidays slid into my life this year on the heels of a hectic schedule and several life changes. I was looking forward to a simple observance with my brother and his family, some visits with friends and, most of all, rest. I kept my expectations in check, however, and was content to simply not be unhappy during the season. My ideal holiday experience was as yet unattainable (parents back home, husband found, children birthed), so I reckoned I had better stick to realism.

As life often does, Christmas Day pleasantly surprised me from its gray morning until its sizzling night. The amazing quality about any given day is how it unfolds gradually, creating issues and conversations that build and crescendo into events that become potent memories for our future. I woke up to drizzly rain, which somehow reminded me of snow and coziness. I lit a "fire" in my faux fireplace and enjoyed its sweet ambience as if the logs were truly burning and crackling before me. I felt optimistic.

I roused my overnight guest, a new little sister, and we prepared for brunch. When my brother and his family arrived, I was laden with unexpected gifts and a palpable sense of peace. From there, I went to a friend's home, where I was showered again with unexpected gifts, food and love. That evening I entered the rambunctious quarters of yet another family I'd known my entire life and met up with a man who'd dined at my home so many times in childhood I almost forgot he actually wasn't my real brother.

Though I hadn't seen him in several years, it was like we'd had dinner together yesterday, except that the stubbly dreadlocks he'd had before had elongated into ropes that wound around his shoulders and cascaded down his back. He had become a rocker and a pescetarian (one who only eats fish and vegetables, I was told) in that time. He stood up to play us a song he had written about forgiveness, and it moved several in the room to tears.

As we all then began to sing everything from heehaw country to old-school gospel, I was moved by the simplicity of friendship through the years, of the ties that bind us to people by blood and by habit, and the joy of being in the presence of those without agendas.

I appreciated the humility of an individual who could use his gifts to encourage and bring joy to others, whether performing before an admiring crowd of influential people or a motley crew of rowdy children and unassuming adults. I thought about my day, so different from the ways I'd spent Dec. 25 in the past, and was grateful that the absence of one kind of celebration had made opportunity for other possibilities. There was an abundance of laughter, tears, music, food and thanksgiving throughout the day. For that I am also thankful, made whole, and ready for even more surprises to come.

PART IV
LOVE AND CONNECTION

"You know you're in love when you can't fall asleep because reality is finally better than your dreams." - Dr. Seuss

31

MIXED MESSAGES

A woman calls her boyfriend before their date.

Woman: "Hey, I was just wondering how I should wear my hair tonight. What do you think, up or down?"

(She's obviously looking for any excuse to call.)

Man answers: "Huh? Either way is fine ... I'm watching the game right now. Why don't I call you back?"

Woman, disappointed: "You're always watching the game. You should spend less time watching TV."

Man, feeling accused: "You should spend less time nagging me about it."

Woman, now hurt: "You know what, let's just forget about tonight. I'm not in the mood."

Man: "What did I say? You're so sensitive!"

Why is communication so difficult? Good communication between genders sometimes requires a miracle. We are not the same, regardless of what some experts say. From birth, males and females behave, react, and learn very differently. And as adults, each of us communicates in what one could almost call our own emotional language. We have different needs.

Psychologist Carol Gilligan was one of the first in her field to highlight fundamental differences between the sexes. She writes that the heart of a man says something like, "I want to enter my world with impact," while the heart of a woman says, "I want to enjoy the world of intimate relationships." A man appreciates being respected and admired while a woman longs to be loved and cherished. Of course this is not to say that women don't want respect or men don't require much love, but we operate predominately out of certain categories of needs.

This impacts how we communicate and interpret what is communicated to us. A man should be careful to communicate in a way that assures a woman she is special. A woman should be careful to always communicate respect to a man. For instance, on a date, relationship guru John Gray says that a man should be careful to compliment a woman directly, making positive comments about her appearance or how fun she is to be with. He should be careful to take care of the little things. Something as simple as walking beside a woman rather than leaving her to fend for herself in a crowd communicates volumes.

A man likes to hear that he's done a good job, that he can make the woman happy. A woman can communicate this by complimenting the date itself, how she liked the movie, or restaurant. She can respond to his efforts to give her a good time by expressing her pleasure, smiling, etc. And advice should be offered only when requested. Now, all this is all good, but sooo much easier said than done. Since I've so often failed in communicating effectively to the opposite gender, I am interested in doing it better. Perhaps when I'm really good, my conversations will go something like this:

Woman: "Hey, just calling to tell you I can't wait to go out with you tonight."

Man: "Really?" (game heard in the background)

Woman: "I know you need to get back to your game, but I just couldn't wait to tell you how much fun we always have. You have such creative ideas. I just appreciate it."

Man turns the TV off. "I can watch the game later. I can't wait to see you either. You are so special to me."

Woman : " See you tonight."

Man: "I can't wait."

32

SLUMBER PARTY FOR GROWNUPS

Pigtailed and glassy-eyed, as little girls we giggled into the night in our best PJs. We pulled out our flashlights under the covers and told funny stories, gorged ourselves on candy and soda, then stayed up late because it was just so thrilling. The young-adult versions were still fun. They included movies, talking, crazy games and, of course, pizza.

My latest slumber-party experience was the best ever. I hosted an overnight event that included Grandma P., an 82-year old widow, Sara (not her real name), a 40-plus divorcee, me, mid-30s, and Zipphora, a 29-year-old newly engaged woman.

We settled down in the living room when our stomachs were full of seafood and sweet drinks. After a round of lighthearted questions, we began to talk freely and laugh as Grandma P. gave us advice on love and marriage.

"Put on a soft glove, even when you're arguing," she said. "Prepare a man for a serious discussion by doing something sweet for him first." Then, "Keep it fun! You don't have to be serious all the time!" she said.

While white candles burned on the coffee table, we reclined on couches and shared accounts of botched romances, enchanted travel trips and the like. As I began to doze, Grandma P. told me firmly to go to sleep. Reluctant to beat an 82-year-old to dreamland, I protested, but finally went off to bed. She quickly followed suit, leaving our fellow party companions awake to linger in chatter, photo swapping and secret-telling.

Morning came in quiet sunlight, and we feasted on sweet bread, fresh fruit, cream and hot tea. Zipphora prepared to go for a morning bike ride with her fiancé, and Grandma P. teased, "Please let us see him before you leave."

Later, when he stepped inside, Grandma P. threw her arms out gleefully, "I know him! Girl, you've got a good man!"

Zipphora and her man smiled proudly before escaping. Still in our nighties, the rest of us continued our conversations, turning to more serious talk of life's disappointments, frustrations and confusing moments. We lamented our mistakes, regrets and wishes for more wisdom.

Grandma P. began to speak about forgiveness. "Forgiveness is like a resurrection," she said. I pondered this deeply, that our regrets could be buried and something completely new could spring from their perpetual rest. We could lay them down and move on. The freedom of this was staggering. By the time we dissolved the party, Sara remarked, "I felt I had been in something like a trapped room, and now I see the doorway out." I was feeling thoroughly encouraged and centered. Zipphora, who had returned, felt enlightened by practical wisdom, and remarked, "Those were great stories."

Grandma P., who had been tired the day before, was invigorated. We parted ways in a flurry of hugs and kisses and promises of yet another slumber party. Tomorrow night wouldn't be too soon.

33

SINGLENESS

Oprah has a column in "O," her popular magazine, titled, "What I Know For Sure." I'll tell you what I know for sure: Being single is not for the faint of heart. At [the time of this writing] I am completely single — meaning I don't even have a significant other. These days even routine scenarios make me painfully aware of my state of being. And nothing, I mean nothing, could have prepared me for this phase of my life. My parents' generation didn't even attempt to because they didn't envision it.

How could my mother coach me on how to emotionally handle the abject fear that I may never marry? She married at 23, right after she finished school. At 23, I had barely had a boyfriend. How could my father know how rejected and lonely I often would feel after years of short-term relationships? He assumed his little girl would have no problems in this area. Who would have thought that a confident, adventuresome girl would grow into a confident, adventuresome woman who is insecure in this very important area: relationships with the opposite sex.

I've wanted to talk about this for a long time. It makes me feel vulnerable, you must know. I am right smack in the middle of the dilemma. A friend and I decided that a single woman over the age of 30 has about the same level of emotional fragility that a man has when he can't find work. It's so difficult for him because working is at the core of who he is. And a woman not married? Well, fill in the blanks.

A woman finds her meaning through close relationships, family being the most important. It doesn't help when well-meaning individuals pick at — I mean inquire about — you with questions such as, "Why aren't you married ... yet?" Or, "Are you seeing anyone ... yet?" It's not that I haven't had dates from quality men. I definitely have. But finding your soul mate is more difficult, at least for some of us. And then there are the normal social realities that few people even think about—weddings, date night type of social functions, even church.

Recently, I was sitting at a meeting with work colleagues when suddenly everyone at the table began showing pictures of children and grandchildren. I realized that I was the only non-married-with-no-children person in the room. This bothered me in a way it hadn't in the past. I felt odd, out of place. Singleness, as a lifestyle, is largely a product of this generation of individuals. We have postponed marriage, lead fast-paced lives that often make community living more difficult, and pour ourselves into careers to replace the meaningfulness that only human relationships can bring. Yet, most singles I know strongly wish to be married one day.

Several weeks ago, I had the privilege of sitting down with singleness guru and author Michelle McKinney-Hammond. She was in town for a speaking engagement, and I just had to meet with her to discuss this overarching issue of our time. A never-married woman herself, Ms. Hammond is beautiful and has a presence that exudes confidence, serenity and purpose. She gave me several insights on living a full and pleasurable single life. I'll share some of them with you: For those struggling with their ticking biological clocks, she says, "Do you want to be a mother (or father) or to simply give birth? There are countless children in need of a father or mother, and you can fulfill part of that need by mentoring, fostering and spending time with others' children.

Never underestimate the importance of rich friendships with the opposite sex. So often we overlook these in our search for romance. Fill your life with meaningful activity. You'll be too tired to be lonely. Remember, while single people are looking to be married, married people often envy the freedom of singles. Learn to enjoy the different seasons of life. Singles often overlook the happiness that is right before their eyes. Spend more time being the right person than simply looking for the right person." Too true. I'll get to work.

34

WAITING FOR MR. RIGHT IS WORTH IT

Most of us hate to wait. When we learned the adage "Good things come to those who wait" in grade school, we assumed the teachers meant waiting for recess, or snack time, or summer vacation. When waiting involves months, years or even decades, we begin to wonder if anything good will ever come. Growing up, P.S. assumed she'd marry right after college and have at least five babies. "I always knew it, but once I started helping with my nieces and nephews, I thought, well maybe I won't have five," she said. (P.S. asked that only her initials be used to preserve her privacy.)

After leaving her home in Alabama, she moved to Tennessee and enrolled in Middle Tennessee State University in Murfreesboro, where she majored in psychology. After a year then spent in New York City, she returned to the South, preferring the pace of life in Chattanooga. Settling into adult life, P.S. enjoyed the company of men (a relative describes her as very cute). Yet, somehow, something always seemed to prevent her from walking down the aisle. Things would go wrong in the relationship before a wedding date could be set, or the situation would crumble before there was even talk of marriage.

"I came close several times but I knew it wasn't the right person. I never wanted a divorce, so I was always very selective and cautious. I never got a ring," P.S. explains. After coasting through her 20s without matrimony, she pushed through the 30s (when she really wanted to marry), and struggled through her 40s (when she really, really wanted marriage), until she finally reached age 50.

Once on the other side of this major life marker, she assumed that marriage must not be her destiny. Her time had come and gone. She had a good life, full of travel and loving friends and a close knit family.

She spent her free time gardening, working around her house and loving people. "I realized I could have a life without being married," P.S. remembers, and finally settled into a place of peace and contentment.

When she began dating her current beau, she wasn't thinking of marriage. In fact, she says, "He came into my life and I told God I was fine as I was. It was weird to think of marriage." He had other ideas, however. A widower, he'd been married for many years prior to meeting P.S. and truly cherished the institution of marriage.

He proposed. She said yes. She has played the waiting game and won. Now, her feelings heading in a totally new direction, she states resolutely, "I believe he is The One beyond a shadow of a doubt. God has set everything up and I just accept it." Her voice takes on an admiring tone as she describes the qualities of her fiancé. She looks forward to spending the next wonderful half of her life with a man she describes as a godly, hard-working, family man. "I'm grateful those other times didn't work out. My advice to single people is to just enjoy life. Forget about what you don't have and enjoy what you do have. Live today to the fullest. Count your blessings."

In just a few days, P.S., age 57, will walk down the aisle for the very first time, a beautiful and radiant and eager bride. Her story proves that good things — even great things — really can and do happen to those who are willing to wait.

35

FINDING JOY AT A SHOWER

Recently I attended one of the best baby showers ever. This is amazing for me to say because I tend to be a bit cynical about the fuss people make over whether to buy pink or blue clothes (the baby doesn't care!), games that force me out of my seat, and ladies who enjoy discussing diaper issues. But when I was asked to decorate for the shower of one of my lifelong and best friends, I didn't hesitate.

I thought of pink roses and brown teddy bears, floating balloons and tiny candles. Her sister, a professional caterer, laid out a spread of comfort foods. A sister-in-law brought the cake. Her mother, undaunted by a broken foot, rolled in sitting in a wheelchair, a willing helper toting a large bag of games behind her. Both my friend's grandmother and grandmother-in-law were in attendance, beautiful and witty. A host of relatives and friends provided extra help and comic relief.

The air was festive. There was a shower crasher, who slunk in late whispering, "I didn't get the invitation, but someone told me about it. Hope it's OK!" And there was an understandably grumpy young boy who sat with a slightly tortured look on his face until an uncle came and picked him up. There was her proud father, who worked the crowd. Ever the jokester, he later remarked with tongue in cheek,

"Well that was my very first shower, so I'm really not sure if I had fun or not."

Her mother's games were surprisingly good, even challenging. In one we popped balloons by sitting on them, and then read the messages that had been hidden inside. We had to guess the prices of baby items and the circumference of my friend's stomach. We then played musical baby doll. If you were holding the doll when the music stopped, you had to put change into a piggy bank or give some baby advice, or both.

A friend once told me about attending an expensive and classy baby shower thrown for a wealthy couple. It had cost thousands of dollars. The stress of buying the right gift, putting in a certain amount of money for the couple, even finding the perfect outfit for the occasional had seemed to overshadow the joy of the coming baby. At this shower, no one cared if you wore jeans and Tshirt or your Sunday best. There were tons of gifts, lots of laughter and teasing, good eats and the often overlooked blessing of shared clean-up duties.

It was all about the celebration of this couple's journey to parenthood. The mother-to-be seemed to glow with life, and we reveled in her joy. The womanly ritual we had all attended countless times in our lives took on meaning yet again. For those moments, the wear and tear of a stressful and imperfect world seemed to fade, and what emerged was a tender circle of light, full of warmth and good wishes.

36

WHY SHE WENT BACK

When the young, the beautiful and the famous show the world that they are just as vulnerable as the rest of us, we sit up and take notice. A bruised face and body, court dates, lost endorsements and public outrage follow. Just when the furor begins to die down a bit, a new development catches the media's eye. The victim is back with her abuser.

The big question is and remains, "Why did she go back?" And more broadly, "Why do women (and men) stay in relationships that hurt?" It's complicated, but here's what some would say:

It might feel normal. Abuse may be something witnessed in childhood that has become the blueprint for adult relationships. If most domestic or romantic relationships seemed to have this element of anger and loss of control, why should theirs be any different? If they simply say, "We had a fight," they probably don't see themselves as victimized.

They're scared. Many victims of domestic and relationship abuse feel that they have lost any real control of their lives. If they leave, perhaps things will get worse — they could be stalked or harmed unexpectedly. If married, they are afraid to lose children, friends and the life they've always known.

They have lost confidence in themselves. They have finally succumbed to the emotional barrage that has accused them of being nothing without the abuser: unwanted, unattractive, unintelligent or incapable of making good and practical decisions — even if others perceive them differently. Their self-esteem has taken a hit, and they may start to believe the outrageous lies they're being fed.

They feel financially and emotionally dependent. Perhaps there really is not enough money or resources to live apart from their partner. They're afraid to be alone and in charge of everything that concerns them.

They're in love. At least that is what they believe love can look or be like. And so they believe the abusers when they tell them they are so sorry and won't do it again. They "understand" them, their childhoods or the pressures that can make them act the way they do. Or worse, they blame themselves.

Though both genders can be abusive, all studies show that men are much more likely to do so. Interestingly enough, many men (and women) who abuse are not considered to be individuals with outrageous tempers in regular life. They often have a strong need to control or dominate another individual. The cycle of abuse is often one that begins with a setup that leads to aggression (verbal/emotional) or violence. The abuser then feels guilty, mainly of getting caught. He (or she) will rationalize his behavior, become normal by being sweet and charming or by acting as if nothing has happened. Then he begins to fixate on the things that his victim has done wrong, what he will do to "make her pay," and he sets her up again. If you find yourself on either end of this cycle, get help immediately. Call a domestic violence help line today.

37

DATING AFTER 60

Dating advice is usually geared toward the young and never-married. What most people don't realize, however, is that half of America's singles are over 40. Of that crowd, those who are 60-plus and dating make up a growing group of interesting and exciting individuals. This group is unique in that they have often already been married, raised children and worked one or more careers. Many are in good health and have a zest for life unseen in previous generations. They love to celebrate milestones, travel to new places and socialize. Take 65-year old Callie, who told me, "My class is going to have a Medicare party soon. We'll eat, drink, and (the ones who can still move) will dance!"

People over 60 aren't necessarily dating with an intention of marriage. Callie said she wants someone to spend time with. "In marriage, the good times outweighed the bad," she said. "You had constant companionship. I'm freer now than in my 30s. I have no kids, no job, so it would be nice to have someone I could go places with who thinks like me."

Having generational compatibility is an important asset in choosing a companion. Callie told me she could remember when Chattanooga only had one television station and exactly when integration happened. A retired educator, she isn't interested in dating a man who could have been her student long ago. She has made other philosophical adjustments.

"I'm willing to date outside my race now," she said. "I'm open to Internet dating because I don't want to go to clubs." She's also tried mature singles groups hosted by churches. A dislike for nightclubs was a running theme among this age group, though most acknowledged they were club goers in their youth. "We need other places to meet people," Callie said.

All those 60 and above are not the same. Julie, 69, is a travel writer who reports on easily accessible vacations spots. She observed, "I have a friend who is in her 80s and has a beau. I think the older generations, those who grew up before the women's liberation movement, seem to pair up more. My age group is more independent out of necessity. I've been married twice and I love men, but I'm not looking. I like not being responsible for someone else's happiness."

Echoing this tendency toward independence is 65-year-old Gerald, who has never married but occasionally goes out with women introduced to him by his married friends. "I did want to marry when I was younger. As a newspaper man, I worked nights and weekends, and 90 percent of those I worked with were single or divorced. It wasn't a career that lent itself to marriage and family.

"I can see that a lot of the ladies I go out with are expecting to be cared for in a certain way. I know I can't provide that for them." He spends time alone, with friends, and on dates, and is content with the rhythm he's found.

Helen, who describes herself as "60 something," saw the Egyptian pyramids not long ago and is planning a Thanksgiving getaway to another exotic location this year. She says it best when she exclaimed, "We deserve some fun too! We need a better way of meeting people. A new relationship will make your quality of life better. You can travel, laugh together, go to the movies, out to eat, or just talk about anything."

She added, "We may look happy, but there's something missing. It's the closeness of the opposite sex." Love, at any age, is a worthy endeavor.

38

CALM AFTER CONFLICT

I once read a story about a couple who got into a passionate fight in the middle of a street in Paris. The man impulsively flew home to the United States ahead of time, while the woman, left alone on their vacation, decided to enjoy the rest of the week. Ten years later, they returned Europe to reminisce and laugh about that low point in their relationship, but they were still together. On the other hand, many a friendship has broken up over cross words, a misunderstanding or even a calm, calculated comment that hit a sore spot in the listener's heart.

Resolving conflict takes guts. Many people would rather face a scary dog on a lonely street than speak honestly and forthrightly about how another person's actions make them feel. Fears of being rejected, ignored, criticized or belittled give many people pause. Others grew up with such explosive anger in their homes that they relate every argument or uncomfortable discussion to failure. They brace themselves for the big boom. The bottom line is few of us are taught how to handle conflict or to see it as useful to improve and strengthen relationships.

Researchers tell us, however, that conflict is normal in healthy relationships. It has to do with a perceived threat more than just a disagreement and often arises out of the differing needs of individuals. One of the first skills needed to handle conflict respectfully is the ability to regulate one's own rising stress levels. Being aware of one's emotions in the moment is also helpful.

There are times I've handled confrontation well, listening to the complaint or anger of another while trying to respond to their unspoken needs. Other times things went south quickly. I became quickly agitated and responded with anger and defensiveness, or I withdrew and refused to continue the conversation as soon as something was said that I considered offensive.

Often, the times that things went well occurred after I had time to prepare for a conversation. When I was tired, overwhelmed, or caught off guard, monitoring myself became a far more difficult task. If you know that the timing of the other person will make your discussion more difficult, suggest talking at a later moment, or take a few seconds to have a silent conversation with yourself, reminding yourself to remain calm and to simply listen for a few minutes before responding.

Another key skill conflict resolution experts say will help diffuse conflict is to pay attention to nonverbal cues, that is, all the communication that is being expressed without words. Clues to deeper issues may be searched out in facial expressions, body language and the tremor and sound of one's voice. Often people use words to express only part of the problem. For example, if someone says, "You never listen to me!" and they are crying, have a frustrated or frightened look, and are standing with their arms crossed, they may mean, "I'm feeling unsure of your love and commitment to me lately. I'm tired and overwhelmed with my life. Would you please reassure me by helping me feel heard and valued right now?"

A diffusing response can be a warm hug or a focused, caring look along with words spoken in a patient tone like, "I'm listening now. Will you please share what's on your mind?" As each person shares, the two may gain a deeper understanding of each of their needs, and repairing work can begin.

39

WOMEN, FRIENDSHIP, AND LIFE

While sitting with a group of women the other day, the conversation moved toward the support that women traditionally offered one another. "We used to gather, you know?" one lady said. "We broke beans together, or we made quilts. And we talked. We just don't do that anymore." All around the table there were nods of agreement and thoughtful silences.

Why don't we gather like in times of old? My mind wandered back to the countless conversations I'd recently had with women inside and outside my office. In the midst of everything else that may have been bothering them, the underlying theme seemed to stay hauntingly similar.

The voices morph together like "…the bills are due and I'm broke and someone keeps breaking in my house and it's all on me and I can't seem to finish school and my kids are misbehaving and I don't have any help and I'm not losing weight and I did something I feel ashamed of and I'm tired and my body hurts and I just feel so alone." "I feel alone" was the general thread that kept weaving through each story. They knew they needed connection but didn't seem to know where to find it, and even when they knew, they often had to rouse tremendous courage to look for it in the company of other women.

Too often trust had been betrayed in close and meaningful friendships — then rejection and retreat eventually won out. Or they were around other women but at times didn't feel connected to them. They were afraid to share their burdens because they feared being judged. These issues cause many of us to put our energy into romantic relationships, but we quickly learn that as wonderful and affirming as men can be, they are not women. They just can't replace a good sisterly gathering.

When women lend their unique ability to comfort, encourage and nurture to a conversation, a room or an event, deep healing often takes place. I've been in these wonderful situations. I let myself be propped up by loving women who knew just what to do and what to say in my time of need. Through them, I learned to take pride in being a woman and to be excited about learning more about how to share that particular type of strength and beauty with others.

Through the years, I've found that being with other women and attending their luncheons, breakfasts or small groups, somehow strengthens me and gives me joy. Reconnecting with old friends brings a literal sense of stability and relief to me. Recently, I received an email from such a friend. We met more than 17 years ago. We'd been apart for a few years but were communicating again. She was apologizing for the extra time she took to reply to my last email. I emailed back, "No apology is necessary. I'm just glad we're still friends."

Emily Rapp, in her article "Transformation and Transcendence: The Power of Female Friendship," writes about what her experience of working with several older women while living overseas taught her, "... Support, salvation, transformation, life: This is what women give to one another when they are true friends, soul friends ... It's what ... women do for one another in real relationships with real consequences in real time, every day, what my friends do for me. We help one another live ..."

40

ON LOVE

Somewhere in the world today, a baby will be born to parents already in love with it. This Saturday the world will light up with passionate couples eager to join their lives together in marriage. A woman makes her daily call to her best friend. A song is written about what makes the world go around — love. Surrounded by it, we bloom like stunning wildflowers. Most of us know that love heals. Life has meaning when we are aware that people care about us. It is our great motivator, the reason we strive to please and attach ourselves to others. Not only can devotion heal us emotionally, it also impacts us physically.

I recently came across a fascinating article about the physical healing power of love. In one researched study in Israel, men who answered "yes" to the question, "Does your wife show you her love?" were less likely to develop stress-related angina or chest pain. In another very interesting experiment, volunteers were given nasal drops infected with one of two types of rhinovirus, which causes the common cold. All the participants receiving the drops were infected with the virus, but those who had stronger social relationships did not develop cold symptoms as frequently. When people fall prey to diseases that can take their lives, sometimes the only thing that separates those who survive the longest from those who quickly pass is their general sense of well-being in the world.

And yet, so many of us have not mastered the ideals of giving and receiving love. I think about my anger over relationships gone sour. I can't stand rejection, but I encounter it more often than I'd like to admit. The next time, I think, I'll be more careful. And my ability to receive love is closed just a little. Over time, we push ourselves into places too small to allow others in. Unfortunately, we can't let much out either. We protect ourselves in an effort to control life. But much of loving is risk.

Unconditional love is something to strive for in every relationship we have. There is something about loving others in this manner that makes us more human, more alive. When we feel loved, we become more beautiful. When we feel beautiful (inwardly), we want to be kind to people — after all, they're no longer a threat to us. This feeling begets actions that ensure others' safety and well-being, a rippling out effect.

Since enduring a couple of hurtful incidents with friends recently, I have been contemplating the role of love in my life. Now, each kind act a person has toward me lights up in my mind. I can see it! I am grateful for those who are committed to loving me. I am inspired to love others with more intensity, more sincerity, less selfishness.

We can heal with thoughtfulness. A warm hug that connotes safety and belonging can last for an entire day. We can love each other with our words, with our eyes, with our actions. Our very lives may depend on it.

PART V
MIND MATTERS

"This feeling will pass. The fear is real but the danger is not."
Cammie McGovern, Say What You Will

41

THERAPY

If you were in a jungle, and your arm was bleeding, infected and about to fall off, you'd probably want to treat it. In fact, there's a book that tells you how. It's called "Where There Is No Doctor." It's fascinating reading. You can learn how to diagnose a bloated stomach, disinfect your water naturally and set broken bones. If you are traveling to a remote area of the planet and can carry very little with you, this book is a must. On the other hand, if you are near civilization and suffering from a physical ailment, close this book and get to the nearest hospital. Of course, you already know that.

Most of us have profound respect for the medical field. We respect the individuals who can prescribe drugs, perform surgery and give instructions on how to care for aches and pains. When it comes to our mental health, however, many of us are not so open. Just the other day I had a good-natured debate with a friend of mine over the value of therapy. He wondered why anyone would pay a person to talk to them. Never mind that this *person* has studied the intricacies of human thought, behavior and various responses to trauma and emotional pain. Disregard the benefit of a professional who may be skilled in using specific techniques to alleviate certain forms of human suffering and inner conflict. According to him, if your "feeling bone" is broken, just fix it yourself.

He's not alone. Many individuals who come into my office at the injunction of court, parental control or agency referral don't feel they need counseling. They are perfectly fine, they say. It's the others, those people who are really ill, who could benefit. However, as my supervisor Gail stated when I asked her opinion on the subject, "Everyone needs counseling. People who aren't mentally ill need it just as much as the mentally ill — for self-insight."

And what good is self-insight? A bunch of froo-froo get-in-touch-with-your-inner-self ridiculousness? No. Gail continued, "To know yourself and to be honest is the most difficult task of all."

"Why not talk to a friend or read a book?" I countered rhetorically.

"A therapist won't let you get away with things the way a friend might. A good therapist will hold a mirror to you." Most of us prefer to live with a certain amount of denial. After all, our defense mechanisms act to protect us from unpleasant thoughts or feelings. We can hide behind polite talk and superficial connections to avoid stating our true responses to others. We can avoid feeling the pain of rejection, insecurity or a broken heart by achieving, controlling or deciding not to feel at all.

Psychotherapists have compared these various ways of maintaining emotional equilibrium to our bodies' constant regulation of temperature, sugar levels and the like. Cause a disruption, and things get mighty uncomfortable.

If one can stand the occasional discomfort and upheaval, the new self-awareness gained can help one stop doing unproductive or destructive things. It may reveal the deeper implications of a long harbored belief or fear. It could be the motivating factor you need to change your inner and outer worlds for a more fulfilling and authentic life.

For those whose healing begins simply with being listened to, counseling can be a soothing balm. For others who lack understanding about a particular issue, therapy can point them in directions they never thought of before. And for those who have a hard time letting down their guard and admitting what is real, it may be the resounding clap of hard truth that snaps them out of their haze. Therapy is not just for those who feel weak. It is used by people who are strong, brave and humble. Dare to look within. An adventure awaits.

42

MEN AND DIVORCE

D ivorce continues to rock the foundation of American marriage, and unfortunately, it's one of the many things we lead the world in. Divorce sometimes seems to impact men in a more intense way than women. The late mediation expert Kathleen O'Connell Corcoran explains it this way, "… Men are usually confronted with greater emotional adjustment problems than women [after a divorce.] The reasons for this are related to the loss of intimacy, the loss of social connection, reduced finances and the common interruption of the parental role.

"Men remarry more quickly than women. Men are initially more negative about divorce than women and devote more energy in attempting to salvage the marriage. Some believe that the justice system is skewed toward women (especially mothers). Men often end up with much less time with their children, and they're stretched financially beyond what is fair or feasible in some cases.

Researchers believe that women, who tend to recognize marital problems faster than men do, have had more time to accept the ending of the relationship. Corcoran believes that women also reach out for help from others more easily and may even experience an increase in self-esteem rather than a drop in their self-worth after a divorce.

Fathers undergoing divorce should know that the more connected they are to their children prior to separation, the better. Research shows that the length and intensity of conflict between parents makes a huge impact on how children manage. Parents who can communicate well with each other and their children will have better adjusted children.

Neil Millar, coach for divorcing and separated dads, gives this advice for managing emotions during this time:

1. Resist the urge to call your [soon to be ex] and tell her anything. If you have children, you have to see them, [but] do it out of the house and away from your ex.
2. Make sure you go for a walk every evening, around 2-3 hours before you go to bed. The fresh air and the physical movement will help lift your spirits, and you may actually begin to resolve things while you're walking.
3. Twice a day, sit in silence for 5-15 minutes. Focus on your breathing, expand your stomach as you breath in, contract it as you breath out. Acknowledge your thoughts and write them down if they are persistent. This is good for relieving stress, both on the brain and the body.
4. Consider mediation, coaching or counseling. Go to mediation to arrive at a fair understanding of how you dissolve things. Get coaching on how you move forward in your life and how you can both work effectively with your kids. Go for counseling if you are unable to resolve your own issues.
5. Try to avoid mudslinging. Try to avoid court; it costs a fortune. Settle the divorce as quickly and simply as possible. Be prepared to give and take in the negotiation.
6. During all the confusion and reorganizing of things, please consider that in every challenge, there is an opportunity for growth. Look for your opportunity.

Men will do well to read about and discuss the potential impact of a divorce beforehand, creating a plan for support and ongoing sources of advice for themselves. Helpful books to help men maneuver during and after a divorce: "Breakup," Leo Averbach," "From Courtship to Courtroom", Jed Abraham," "A Man's Feelings, Finding Closure After Divorce," Michael Eads.

43

TRAUMA

Years ago, while writing in my bedroom one night, I was caught off-guard by a rap on my window.

"Who is that?" I asked, almost laughing. I thought perhaps a friend was outside playing, attempting to scare me. The rap quickly became a pounding, and somehow the sound took on emotion — no longer a benign knocking, the now angry force menacingly continued. I heard myself screaming, there was the shattering of glass, and then dead silence. A policeman arrived within minutes of my 911 call, letting me know that it looked like the work of mischievous teenagers.

"I don't think they were trying to break in, just scare you," he reported. They had run away when the outer pane of the window shattered. With that knowledge, I relaxed slightly. But later I could not sleep. When my sister-in-law and brother offered to sleep over, I heartily took them up on it. I drifted between sleep and consciousness, tense and hyper alert, literally able to hear the raindrops softly hitting the grass outside. Each flicker of light on the ceiling brought me to full wakefulness, and I cringed when I recalled the overpowering horror and dread that filled me when I did not know if my very life was in danger.

It was the emotion, not the facts, that my soul remembered. Though my mind grasped that what had happened was born of stupidity and youthful ignorance, I still reverberated with the anxiety of vulnerability. For the next several weeks, I struggled with fears abnormal for my usually bold sensibilities. I dreaded the dark, being alone, even sleeping. I felt threatened, even when no one was near me.

I longed for a way to crawl into some sort of protective womb and remain there until life was safe again. I reasoned with myself, journaled and prayed. I realized that I would have to fight the fear, as my aunt had reminded me, or it would take over. I rearranged my room, gave myself certain goals, and proceeded slowly and deliberately. Through the help of many supportive people, I was able to resist the temptation to shrink back from life and eventually recovered fully.

And that was what was required to overcome a rather simple trauma. Many individuals suffering from anxiety disorders, irrational fears, and the like, have had to overcome much more than a few seconds of fear. Rape, violent death, the loss of children, can cause individuals to pull so far into their symbolic wombs that they never want to re-engage with the outside world again.

One woman told me that soon after her best friend died in an automobile accident, she found it difficult to drive. Now, years later, her friends and family often take her places. She suffers from anxiety attacks. She rarely socializes outside her home, and is even ambivalent about romantic interests.

Fear and trauma are not only stored in our minds, they are literally lodged in our bodies. There are stories of individuals having new memories after having heart transplants — often these memories corroborate with the life of the donor. Our bodies react to cues that may take our minds much longer to sort through.

The way out of the prison of fear is a careful plodding. One must be willing to ask for help, take baby steps for change, and feed one's mind with reassurance. It's possible to move to new emotional places. It's often helpful to journal, to nurture one's spirit through pleasant music, art and anything beautiful and uplifting. Change in one's surroundings can help lift the atmosphere. Because fear can grow if left unchecked, pressing forward is an absolute key to recovery. Never give up hope that things can change. Every day is new and can be brighter.

44

SHAME ON YOU!

I was wondering the other day, "Whatever happened to good, old-fashioned shame?" Not the kind that makes a person feel worthless or defective but the sort of shame that regulates one's behavior. One source says that "to 'have shame' means to maintain a sense of restraint against offending others, while to 'have no shame' is to behave without such restraint." We live in an age, a society and among a generation of people who seem to be losing all sense of shame. We see it in their choices of clothing, music lyrics, media antics and in the messages sent through the cyber world.

Not only that, intemperance is emerging in how we settle disputes on the school yards, how we address authority figures or strangers and in who ends up caring for children. Anything and everything just doesn't and shouldn't go. There is a standard out there that humans should try to meet. It means that if certain rules are grossly violated, you should feel, well … ashamed of yourself for it.

I'm not suggesting we all dress or act in some sort of robotic fashion. But I'm glad a mature gentleman on "American Idol" came up with the song, "Pants on the Ground" to express his frustration with seeing so many adolescent boys going about with sagging jeans. He even goes as far as to chant, "You're lookin' like a fool with your pants on the ground!" I think somebody had to say it.

On the same note, a friend of mine tried to discuss his nephew's problematic and extra low-riding jeans with him, asking him how he felt about how others may view him. The nephew said others' thoughts about him did not bother him at all, and he felt no shame about it. My friend was incredulous. "What do you do with a child that feels no shame?"

I've seen children caught in some pretty compromising situations by their own parents. The acts themselves weren't nearly as surprising as their calm, collected responses to being found out. They weren't embarrassed. They didn't care much that they'd disappointed those who loved them. They were sometimes indignant about receiving consequences. They had no idea that they had even violated a behavioral standard. They felt that they had simply made a choice others (their parents) didn't always agree with.

It's true, we can't live our lives by the mantra, "What will people think?" But we surely also can't swing so far the other way that we behave as if we're living on a private island that follows us wherever we go either. Somehow, we must discuss limits, appropriateness, general social norms, thoughtfulness, civility, and even modesty with our children.

Our culture is highly individualistic and prides itself on self-expression. This is a wonderful thing, but let's not forget that sometimes, it's OK to hold something back for the sake of another. To consider time, place, and person. To monitor our impulses and think about why we want to do what we really want to do at that moment. It's why grandma used to say, "Shame on you!" and sometimes, we needed to hear it.

45

JOBLESSNESS

Lisa (not her real name) had been crying the day we talked. "This job thing is just wearing me down," she explained. "People don't know how awful it is not to have a job. People (who have jobs) never think it could happen to them. People think they are smarter, they'll know someone, they would never get caught up in this." Lisa and I exchanged e-mails for a couple of weeks over this dilemma. She thought I should write about joblessness. She had a lot to say.

"No matter how high the unemployment is, if you don't have a job, people still think there's something wrong with you. ... I have never been so depressed in all my life. I've got a college degree, and I can't get a job at JCPenney."

She said she knew people who have gotten so discouraged they just stopped looking for work. "I apply for 10-15 jobs a week," she said.

"I do everything I'm supposed to do, like send thank-you cards, etc., and then I see the job in the paper again. It's incredibly frustrating. If you're a woman and you don't have money, you feel even more powerless, like you're living at someone else's mercy. Men? Their families are depending on them." There's also the embarrassment.

"People ask, 'You don't have a job yet?' " Lisa has observed that though many homeless people have counselors, support groups and programs to help them find jobs, there seems to be nothing of the sort for people like herself. I asked what would encourage her the most. She said, "To know that I'm capable and smart, to know that someone's going to hire me." We began to brainstorm tips that people could use to manage their journeys through joblessness.

Some thoughts:

1. Keep a journal as a stress reliever. If you really enjoy writing, consider starting a blog as a way to chronicle helpful and not so helpful strategies, gain perspective and encourage others.
2. Inform every person you know you are looking for a job. Even the cashier at the store may know something or someone.
3. Try to lay aside any embarrassment or shame about this. Remember, it could happen to anyone.
4. Consider going back to school. (If debt is an issue, research possible grant programs.)
5. Parlay an interest/passion into a way to make supplemental income. (Hire yourself out to sing, write, assist someone in a small business, plan parties, clean houses, baby sit animals and children.)
6. Volunteer for organizations you might like to work for, a great way to meet key people, build relationships and keep yourself from going stir crazy.
7. Do something that causes you to stand out in the job-search jungle. Organize an event with a cause; make sure there's something interesting and unique on your resume.
8. See a counselor, support group or start one of your own to help keep your emotional head above water. Write positive statements on your bathroom mirror to help you stay focused.
9. Find an interesting hobby to fill out your day; let yourself feel the success of being good at it in your own way.

I noticed that Lisa used lots of examples, colorful language and was highly expressive throughout our interview. As it turns out, Lisa is also a great writer. She intends to begin to make use of this talent in the coming weeks along with other items on the list. All the best to her and so many others out there. Keep believing.

46

WHAT I'VE LEARNED FROM CLIENTS

The world of a counselor can seem strange to others. We are often privileged to enter the most personal of people's worlds and then, after about an hour, to exit. We work alongside clients — brave individuals who are often fighting their hardest for change — hoping to provide insight and honest feedback (but not too honest), all the while praying our own mistakes don't wound them any further.

It's a delicate balance of humility and confidence. The catalyst for therapy is often an insatiable curiosity about humanity and what makes us all tick. For all the things we therapists and counselors want to teach, however, we often find ourselves learning so much more. Here are just a few things my amazing clients have taught me over the past 12 years:

It ain't over till it's over. I've seen the most wonderful turnarounds. I've watched people head towards a sure relationship breakup after weeks and months of fighting seemingly unsolvable dilemmas, then suddenly encounter a breakthrough of communication or insight that causes them to fall in love again. Sometimes complex problems are solved in the simplest of ways. A person can come in with a long list of complaints, do one thing differently — I mean as small as eating more vegetables — and watch several issues begin to resolve.

Life and people can be startlingly unpredictable. You can't always tell by the paperwork about the particular resiliency, flexibility and passion of the person who wants to change. People surprise you, no matter how long you work with them. Sometimes it's a good thing, other times, not so much. Roll with it.

Being victimized rivals plain old loneliness. Loneliness is just one of the hardest burdens of humanity. We severely underestimate the need for love and connection and the importance of ridding isolation from our lives.

Children can grasp many of the same concepts as adults, and sometimes at deeper levels. I'll never forget an adolescent girl who struggled with panic and anxiety. I talked with her about her perspective of the world, had her draw a picture of her panic attack to see what it looked like, taught her deep breathing, etc. She got better, and I mean fast. She grabbed hold of every technique and ran with it. She was such an inspiration to me.

You're never too old (and it's never too late) for change. One woman completely reinvented herself in retirement when faced with financial difficulties, health problems and a changing identity. She went back to school and chose a completely new career while she was in her 60s. She is still making plans.

Vulnerability, transparency and authenticity make people more beautiful. Some people wouldn't dare venture inside a counselor's office. They're frightened by the prospect of someone examining their less-desirable parts. The truth is, however, that staunch self-protection can be a turn-off. People who let you inside the mess are endearing. They become more beautiful, not less, because of their courage.

Mistakes happen. Forgiveness helps covers them. Ah! The torment of regret, of lost love, angry words poorly spoken, or missed opportunities … how they sting us. We have to learn to give grace to ourselves so we can pass it on to others.

Tears are sometimes the best response. I've sat across from a few clients with no clever antidote to the painful story that just escaped their lips while tears coursed down their cheeks. Despite my best efforts, because I don't cry easily, I found myself joining in. Sometimes words are unnecessary. Compassion is enough.

47

CHANGING FROM THE INSIDE OUT

Humans, by nature, are prejudiced. To those who are shocked by this fact of life, perhaps I can explain it this way: We all have a preference for certain groups or people over others. Some of us prefer to spend time with people of a certain religious or even denominational leaning; others feel most comfortable with people of a particular socio-economic class. The majority of us feel most comfortable around people who share our particular cultural context.

Living is a largely subjective experience. Our personal lives are full of histories, experiences, beliefs and subconscious workings that often make interpersonal objectivity a fleeting idea. Most people say they are not prejudiced. However, social scientists would beg to differ — and have repeatedly. In the landmark book "Emotional Intelligence," by Daniel Goleman, social psychologist Thomas Pettigrew says, "The emotions of prejudice are formed in childhood, while the beliefs that are used to justify it come later. ... You may want to change your prejudice, but it is far easier to change your intellectual beliefs than your deep feelings. Many [white] Southerners have confessed to me, for instance, that even though in their minds they no longer feel prejudice against blacks, they feel squeamish when they shake hands with a black [person]. The feelings are left over from what they learned in their families as children."

Studies recent and historic have outlined with dolls, pictures and mock scenarios how perceptions of people who look certain ways are developed in children as young as 4 and 5 years old. They are often acting out of unspoken emotional influences, subtle behavioral codes and, on some occasions, the overt modeling from the adults around them.

Most human communication is nonverbal, which helps explain why people often sense if they are welcome or not, or if someone feels uncomfortable, nervous or angry in their presence — even when they speak in what appears to be a relaxed, open and friendly manner.

So what do we do with these internal and often subconscious perceptions that often guide us? Goleman, who believes that addressing our hidden prejudices is an important way to grow in emotional intelligence, believes that simply putting people of different backgrounds together does little to eradicate deep-seated prejudice. He suggests doing something like the following:

We must become aware of our propensity to see people subjectively and act in open and non-prejudiced ways despite our knee-jerk feelings. We must not tolerate prejudice. When one person makes a negative remark or slur about a particular group, it seems to prompt others to do the same. One can change the atmosphere of any dialogue by moving the focus back to positive ground. One can also speak out against prejudice in any communal setting.

Working together toward a common goal seems to do more to break down walls than anything else. For example, those who participate in multicultural sports teams, diverse groups that promote social equality, heterogeneous military campaigns, etc. seem to more easily address and melt away their prejudices. We must remember that having a diversity of thoughts and perceptions around us will only enhance our work, learning and living environments.

Our recurring national controversies concerning race, religious, gender and other orientations provide opportunities for us all to take a long, hard look at our inner landscapes and courageously work toward change from the inside out.

48

FACING THE STRAIN OF OVEREATING

I've plumped up over the years. The reasons are complex and mysterious.

Part of it is a rapidly slowing metabolism, another side is stress, a section of the problem is most likely hormonal, while yet another component is due to the additives and vitamin depleting processing that we find so normal for the food we eat in these dear old United States.

The most insidious issue, however, is probably my drama-filled, on-again-off-again relationship with simple carbohydrates and sugar. Conquering these fiends, which I sometimes mistake for *friends*, takes courage and the stamina of an addict bent on recovery. I recently listened to renowned eating disorder specialist, storyteller, and writer Dr. Anita Johnston tell the story of a woman who met a special someone named Chip — as in Chocolate Chip. Their courtship and dating life were fabulous, but she quickly became obsessed with him. Her friends could see that he was no good for her, and finally she gave him up. They're still cordial when they run into each other at the supermarket, but that mysterious pull is gone. She's free of him.

Johnston, a regular lecturer at Focus Healthcare, offered this humorous illustration as an example of how she helps individuals see their struggles with food in metaphorical terms. Most of us can relate to loving someone who is just all wrong for us. We know what it's like to enjoy something in the moment while heaping more problems on our lives at the back end. That's what compulsive eating sometimes offers us — immediate relief from a long and stressful day, relaxation, comfort and the numbness of not feeling.

Compulsive overeating, though not generally seen as immediately life-threatening as anorexia or bulimia, can still be a disruptive life issue. The struggle to maintain a normal weight presents various problems. Self-esteem can be compromised if the overeating also leads to obesity. And then there's the shame, the secrecy, the hiding.

People sometimes eat past the point of satisfaction to stuff down unwanted memories from the past, to shield themselves from uncomfortable emotions, to protect themselves by adding layers, to avoid dealing with life's pressures.

Sugars and carbohydrates can stoke chemical fires in the brain that create a rush of euphoria. After going without refined sugar for several days, I ate a small cup of cookies and cream ice cream after a healthy lunch. I literally felt a burst of happiness travel through my body and up through my head. I was high on sugar. I had never been so aware of what I was seeking when I ate decadent and nutty chocolate or reveled in my boxes of Whale Crackers. I was after that sense of well-being, escape and fun.

Unfortunately, the euphoria fades to frustration when your pants don't button. So you try again. Johnston would say that you must understand your underlying needs, the unique symbolism in what you are doing, then learn the tools to moving past your barriers to get to the other side. Freedom is on the other side. It's when you, like the woman in the story, can pass your own beloved food without losing your mind, yet still behave cordially.

The temptation may be to ramp up our efforts in rigid rules, but that isn't the goal. Balance is the key. Food brings life, is meant to be enjoyed and is good like medicine when used in right portions and with good intentions.

For resources on the subject of compulsive overeating, visit *www. allianceforeatingdisorders.com.*

49

POSITIVE THINKING

Positive thoughts don't come naturally. Often, we're too busy thinking about what went wrong or what might go wrong. These thoughts stress us out and sometimes make us sad. Scientists tell us, however, that our thoughts have the power to affect our mood and emotions. It takes practice to make uplifting thoughts our first response.

The benefits of positive thoughts, however, are vast. In one study, these types of thoughts seemed to help a person increase overall life satisfaction, reducing anxiety and depression and seeming even to help them improve physical health and reduce their risk of mortality.

Therapists call this Cognitive Behavioral Therapy (CBT). Our cognitions, or thoughts, often get stuck in negative patterns. These habitual grooves cause us to go around and around in circuits that cause us to tell the stories of our lives in certain ways. For example, these grooves may cause us to see ourselves as victimized, angry, entitled, depressed or defeated. We feed ourselves these thoughts and interpretations, and we feel the same way day after day.

Many of these thoughts, though originally based on facts, have become distorted. In a classic self-help book called "Feeling Good," by David D. Burns,, the author helps readers identity their cognitive distortions and come up with more reality-based and positive perspectives on the truth of their situation. These new ways of thinking help break the willing person out of mental patterns that have caused emotional patterns that have often led to negative behavioral patterns.

Here are some practical ways to change our thinking:

1. For unpleasant and intrusive thoughts: One simple technique that often helps is to block unpleasant thoughts or images is to say "Stop!" loudly and clap your hands once.

   Over time, if the thoughts or images return, hopefully less frequently, you can simply think "stop." Quickly change to a new activity or focus on a different, more uplifting thought after each episode.

2. Disappointment:
   Allow yourself at least a few hours or even days to fully engage in your sad, frustrated or painful feelings. At the end of that time, begin to think of ways the situation could have been much worse, or what life circumstance you might find more distasteful than the event you endured. Next, come up with something to be grateful for about the situation. Did it teach you character? Did it build your emotional muscles in some way? Can you relate to a friend in a new way?
   This can be done repeatedly.

3. Performance anxiety: Do you become weak in the knees when you think about the speech, exam or presentation facing you? Performance anxiety is a powerful stealer of sleep and emotional comfort in the days prior to the event.
   Try focusing on a place of pleasant escape while breathing calmly, and visit this place to take a break from the obligations in your real life.

4. Feeling tense and stressed: Practice mindfulness, which is considered a walking meditation that simply requires that you keep your thoughts in the present moment. Notice nature around you, people passing, your own body sensations, your senses. Savor the events of right now.

5. The past has you down: Remember that your future is still waiting on you, untainted and full of possibilities. Since we don't know exactly what it will hold, we may as well imagine the best. Even if it doesn't happen exactly the way we picture it today, we just may get closer than we expected.

50

REWRITING OUR STORIES

Everyone loves a good story. We love to hear them, and we love to tell them. Sometimes they come out a little garbled, like the ones my niece Hannah would tell when she was only 3 or 4 years old. She'd get so excited and animated, but we wouldn't know what in the world she was talking about. Others stories are epic, told to children of various cultures and time periods over centuries.

We all have a story. Our personal stories are a combination of truth, perspective and, sometimes, good old-fashioned fiction. We often choose what we want to emphasize in the yarns we weave about our lives, and that affects how we live. I read an interesting article a couple years ago about the fact that sometimes we needed to tell new stories about our lives, ones that made them work better. Sometimes our old, stale stories hold us back.

So, I've got a story to tell, and it's rather short. I've been telling myself that I'm not a very organized person for years. I knew I had certain bursts of what I like to call brilliance in this area, but they seemed short-lived. Then I'd fade back to my normal, disorganized status quo. Well, several people have done my taxes over the years, and at least two of them mentioned how organized my materials were. The first time I was told this, I quickly shrugged it off. "No, I'm not organized at all." I wondered if he were just being polite.

The next person who told me said it emphatically, "You just don't know. I've seen people bring their materials in a bag and drop them on my desk." I thought, well compared to that, I guess I'm organized. Then I kept thinking about it. What if I really were more organized than I'd believed all these years? What more could I be accomplishing if I believed that I could work through things systematically? What confidence could I have about accomplishing my goals? I reflected on the fact that I love organizing things into files and notebooks, finding places for things to go, and cleaning up clutter.

I was stunned. That old story had impacted my life in such a negative way. My behavior had often become a self-fulfilling prophesy. I decided it was time to switch to a new story. In this one, I really was able to accomplish things because I really was somewhat organized. If I made a mistake, it was just that — a mistake, not a pronouncement that I was incapable of getting myself together. I felt excited about the possibilities.

Recently, I gave a friend a compliment about her looks. She immediately rejected it and began complaining about her pants. I became indignant, "I gave you something and I want you to accept it!" Everyone around me began to laugh at my passionate response. But I knew that if she kept telling herself a negative story about her looks, it could affect her in ways she hadn't considered.

What's your story? Is it one in which bad things always happen to you and there's nothing you can do about it? Or is it uplifting and full of gratefulness and wonder? Whatever you're telling yourself is directly linked to your perception of life, your abilities, and the joy you may or may not be experiencing. So if your story isn't working, start writing a new one. It doesn't have to be long, one sentence will do. The results might just amaze you.

51

TIPS FOR BUILDING CONFIDENCE

Self-confidence. If it could be reduced to a potion and drunk from a bottle, many of us would buy it. Building it takes time, perseverance, energy. In a recent conversation, I was asked how one goes about developing more of it. I gave a couple of suggestions but found myself curious. What exactly does go into creating a confident person, especially one who must conjure much of it up for himself or herself later in life? If you're tired of sitting on the sidelines while others are diving into life, keep reading. Here's what some of the experts have to say about creating it the homemade way:

- Understand the connection between unconditional self-love/ self-acceptance and higher performance.

    When we choose not to compare ourselves with others but to appreciate our own uniqueness, we can develop a sense of confidence from knowing we have something to offer the world in a way that is uniquely ours.

    Loving ourselves means forgiving ourselves for making mistakes, being patient with our imperfections and showing compassion for our own weaknesses. Love helps us walk in grace with ourselves as well as with others. Love is a powerful energy force. When we use it, it makes us better humans.

- Draw toward people who are affirming and supportive. One of the things I've learned along the way is that linking up with a positive group of almost any kind helps me build self-confidence and love. Today, I am almost always part of such a group and, when I am not, I will actively seek one out. It can be a group that centers around spiritual connection, professional pursuits, emotional support, hobbies or skills, etc. So long as the people take the time to meet regularly and encourage each other, it will have a dazzling effect on your confidence.
- Start with goals you know you can accomplish. Sometimes my goals are to simply clean my kitchen and vacuum my bedroom. Once those are done, I feel I can tackle more-daunting tasks. Doing the small things also has a way of creating enough space in your brain to imagine and work on the things you really want to accomplish in life.
- Take action quickly. Fighting procrastination is just plain tough. Often, when we struggle with confidence, the fear of failure or the dread of the difficult keep us ruminating over a task that just needs to get done now. If we would take action with some part of it, however, it would help us to move toward its completion, causing us to breathe more easily and feel a sense of pride.
- Tend to your health and appearance. It's not that looks are everything, but they are something. Experts tell us that when we take time to eat healthy, exercise and present our best possible selves to the world, we just feel better. This glow can in turn cause others to respond to us in positive ways, which builds our confidence.
- Remember that you are not the sum of others' opinions about you. This is tricky. People can offer useful feedback to help us grow. But sometimes we still rehearse destructive statements offered to us in childhood from peers — and worse — sometimes our own families, that have damaged us and stunted

our self-esteem. Negative, unloving statements keep us from reaching our fullest potential. Remember that the voice of love is affirming, even if it is corrective. Throw out voices that are not honoring of you as a human being and don't acknowledge your ability to change and grow throughout life. Setbacks are normal, so congratulate yourself on each accomplishment, no matter how small.

52

SENSE OF ADVENTURE

My parents are at it again. They were on the lookout for a new adventure and, sure enough, they've found one. After a whirlwind interview and observation weekend at an international boarding school last month, they have accepted the position of house parents there. They aren't exactly sure how much energy they'll need each day to deal with high-spirited, often homesick teenagers, but they're willing to give it a try. They are great examples of people who live life to the fullest, without regrets.

Living an exciting life takes effort and courage. One of my best friends loves to travel and has utilized creative avenues to do so, finding journalism, religious and educational grants to help pave the way. Once, when I couldn't locate her by cell phone for several days, I contacted her family, feeling a little worried. They tracked her down in Iceland. Iceland!? I remembered that she'd mentioned wanting to visit the country while she was on a stopover from a trip to Europe. I had no idea she'd actually made plans to make it happen.

The key to living life this way has to do with one's mindset. One must choose it. I've spoken to more people than I care to remember who are afraid to venture outside the familiar. Even though they find their lives strangely unsatisfying, they prefer convention over the new, the mundane over the exciting, the familiar over a mindboggling experience.

But if you're looking to spread your wings even in just small ways, here are five ways to begin:

Find out what makes you feel alive. This can be service to others, travel, creative pursuits, almost anything. Mind-altering substances aren't needed when one gets a high from living out the things he or she feels born to do.

Take initiative. One of the most surprising discoveries I have made about adulthood is that the things I dream about won't happen unless I leave the house and put forth some effort. Let the first few steps be small. They get bigger as your courage grows.

Accept the fact that sadness and setbacks are as much a part of life as joyful moments. Many people get stuck when tragedy strikes. Deep in their subconscious mind they knew pain existed but didn't think it would happen to them. When we understand that death, pain and heartache come with the territory of living, then pain, though devastating, won't last quite as long.

Be optimistic. This means that, even when feeling down, expect to feel up again eventually. When you are able to find meaning and lessons to learn in the difficult moments of life, the journey deepens.

Minimize the meaning of failure. Every time we take a risk, we look the possibility of failure in the eyes and put up a fight. If he wins one round, we take him for another. Finally, we build up the mental muscles to win.

Remember, those who seem to smile the most are often those who have chosen to live freely, with a sense of wide-eyed openness to the world and its possibilities. This can be done in small, everyday ways as well.

It can be the act of driving through a new neighborhood to find out what's there, taking an enrichment class just because it's interesting or making friends with a new type of person just to broaden oneself and reach out to another. Just follow the sense of excitement and feelings of fulfillment.

53

THANKFUL FOR A LIFE OF GROWTH

In the summer of my 13th year, I grew about three inches in height. I enjoyed the surprise of my growth spurt, the attention it brought me through the exclamations and smiles of the adults in my world. It made the general craziness of puberty bearable. I felt proud and excited about what was to come. Personal growth is a lot like that. We enjoy it after the fact, because it makes the wildness of life somehow worth it all. Today, I am most grateful for occasions life tossed my way that, in the moment, made me want to duck and dodge but produced a wonderful expansion of my soul later on.

I'm thankful for the people who didn't always like me. At the time, the rejection and loneliness I felt were not pleasant, but after I allowed myself to cry it out, work through my sensitivities and try different methods to make peace with others, I learned a lot about myself. In some cases, I discovered that I was deeply enjoyed and highly regarded, but due to my own filtered lenses, had made up stories about my life that simply weren't true. What a relief it was to know that things were better than I thought in some situations. In others, I learned to give myself grace.

I am thankful for my many embarrassing moments. My fiascos have provided comic relief to the heavier moments of my life. Some great stories that kept people laughing for days came out of them. Embarrassment taught me not to take myself too seriously. It keeps me guessing about what may happen next. I can't express how grateful I am that I took risks. I went to college far from home and only came back twice a year. It got hard and even ugly at times, but I eventually graduated and have few regrets.

I'm glad I joined the Peace Corps after college and lived overseas, and though I decided on three occasions to give up and return to the States during my two-year tour, I changed my mind each time and stuck it out. Later, I started a business, and found it much like giving birth to a baby that isn't sure it wants to be born, yet in the end makes you (almost) forget the pain. I wrote my thoughts down and let others read them. I wrote my thoughts down again and spoke them aloud to groups of people. Today, the inner doors these risks opened for me shine like magnificent jewels along my path.

In contrast, I am grateful for my lost opportunities. They filled me with sadness and regret, teaching me that life is short, and that if you don't move on certain things, eventually someone or something else will. They force me forward. And what would I have done without life's surprises? Some weren't pleasant — like the letter that denied me entrance to graduate school. Others were more palatable, like an opportunity to visit Asia free of charge. I smile when I realize that though it's important to plan, you just never know sometimes.

Lastly, I am forever and ever grateful for undeserved love. I am amazed that I have parents who have never divorced, for friendships that have lasted since childhood, for forgiveness and understanding when I've acted my worst.

Love is the beacon we all search for to guide us. It is the force behind all our growth, and everything that means anything. Today, I am thankful that love covers my mistakes, infuses every confusing moment, and cushions my disappointments. It has moved me past puberty and into adulthood and keeps me growing ever still.

EPILOGUE

Dear Readers:

One of the reasons I like the Hello Kitty brand is that I prefer hellos to goodbyes most all the time. That cat seems to always be announcing a new day with a bright, happy face — and I don't even like cats. That's powerful.

There are many hellos to experience in this life. They stand like open doors, inviting us to walk through them into new relationships, new jobs, new experiences. My hello to column writing came as a result of a deal I made with a friend who was mad at me for taking a hiatus from writing.

I've enjoyed writing my whole life. I'd send friends and family humorous letters, write short stories about funny life events or expound on my intense feelings about social or personal issues. When this paused, she exhorted me to begin to write again. I told her teasingly she needed to return to some things in her life as well, like school. So she went back to school, and I presented my clips to the Chattanooga Times Free Press. It was a good hello for both of us. She completed a degree. I began this column.

This one hello has made a huge impact on my life. I've had opportunities to express myself through writing on a regular basis. I've met wonderful people, spoken to groups of individuals and made fun media appearances.

Sadly, however, the time for goodbye has come. Twelve years later, I am thinking of new ways to express my heart and mind. I am hoping for new beginnings in my career, in the location of my work, in my outlook on life.

I've thought of what I will have to leave behind, and I've hated to do it. I have reflected on the need to let go of certain things in order to grab hold of new ones. We can't carry every-thing at once in life. When we try, we end up dropping them like excessive grocery bags. We have to choose certain things to carry, then lay those down, pick up a few more, and so on. We get to experience them better this way, savor them.

And so, I am laboring to let go.

I have reluctantly let go of relationships that had run their course, thought patterns that were hurting me, habitual be-haviors that weren't helping me. I fought myself to see them off, but when I did, new people, new ways of seeing and thinking, new opportunities began to emerge.

So, today, I am saying goodbye to this column. I so appreciate you for reading it, sharing your comments and appreciating (or not) my thoughts. I thank the paper for giving me such an opportunity and my editors for helping me sound better through the years. I have been honored and humbled by this platform. It has been an amazing experience. Please look for me in new places. I would love to write more about travel, spin an interesting series now and then, or share some re-views. You have been more than gracious to me, and I can't thank you enough. I hope we keep in touch.

Love, your humble columnist-turned-writer at large,
Tabi

So I said goodbye to one phase of my writing career. This book is written as a thank you to my readers, who humbled me with their enthusiasm and loyalty, and to my family and friends, who believed in me then and believe in me now. Together, let's turn and face our many waiting hellos.

ACKNOWLEDGEMENTS

I want to thank God for giving me a love for and gift of writing. He has opened many unlikely opportunities to express myself. Thank you to my father J.C. and my mother Janice, who lamented the ending of my column and have waited with baited breath for this book to arrive. I also want to thank my sister Rowena Williams and my brother Travis Upton for enjoying my writing since I was a little girl.

To my supportive friends and extended family who have loved to read my thoughts in various ways through the years, you can never know how much this meant to me. For fear of leaving someone out, I won't try to name you all here, but you know who you are. Thank you to my third grade teacher, who didn't remember me when I saw her again as an adult, but who had told another teacher in my hearing that I was a good writer. Without that comment, I'm not sure I would have taken myself seriously enough to continue.

Many thanks to Mark Kennedy for hearing me out when I first walked into his office looking for a freelance opportunity, for giving me this column, and for ultimately naming it. Thank you, editor Shawn Ryan and the staff at Chattanooga Times Free Press, for allowing me to write it for as long as I desired. Thank you readers, who spoke and wrote kind words to me continuously and whose comments and emails gave me the courage to continue.

Made in the USA
Middletown, DE
18 September 2016